BUILD LIKE THE BIG PRIMES

A Contractor's Guide To Building Your Business While Balancing Your Life

MICHAEL RIEGEL

INDIE BOOKS
INTERNATIONAL

The Build Like the Big Guy Toolbox™ is a pending trademark of Michael Riegel.

ISBN-10: 1-952233-07-0
ISBN-13: 978-1-952233-07-4
Library of Congress Control Number: 2020904439

Designed by Joni McPherson, mcphersongraphics.com

INDIE BOOKS INTERNATIONAL, INC
2424 VISTA WAY, SUITE 316
OCEANSIDE, CA 92054
www.indiebooksintl.com

To Deborah, who has supported me throughout my career and has allowed me to experiment in developing my own style, approach, and perspective. You have been and continue to be my greatest fan and supporter, even when you had no earthly idea what I was talking about.

To Jacob and Sophie, who have always asked for help and shown appreciation for creative, novel, and unique approaches to solving problems. I am more proud of how you have grown and matured than of any professional accomplishment.

CONTENTS

PREFACE

When I was a kid, my favorite toys were LEGOs and Tinker Toys, followed by Erector sets and model airplanes. Later, my father would have me help him around the house with minor home repairs (some of which went well, and some we've agreed not to bring up again). I would admire the collection of tools hanging on the wall, neatly arranged like some sort of industrial artwork. The sight of a construction project on the streets would slow my pace as I would watch the heavy equipment move earth, place concrete, or deliver materials.

If I'm being honest, I still get that feeling when I see construction and often succumb to the urge to stand and watch the interplay of workers and machines on a busy construction site.

When my parents realized I had an aptitude for working with tools, they suggested I might enjoy going into dentistry. Despite the fact that dentists have a lot of really cool tools, I took a pass on that idea. Why? First of all, most people loathe the idea of going to the dentist, and I didn't want to be a part of something that instills fear. Second, I wasn't interested in spending years studying hard sciences.

While I knew what I *didn't* want to do, I found that it took a crooked and wandering path to lead me to what I *did* want to do. I began to accumulate a different set of tools I found helpful in building—not construction projects, but businesses and organizations.

Today as a coach, speaker, and consultant to small businesses, I am keenly aware of the two sets of tools I continue to expand upon. I still like getting my hands dirty and the smells and sounds of construction as I complete my own projects. The physical toolbox increases with each new project and when the need arises for some piece of specialty equipment, such as an offset wrench or radial arm mitre saw. The mental toolbox continues to grow with a personal attitude of being a lifelong learner—learning from articles, books, magazines, experiences, and colleagues. What I've found to be the most satisfying has been the opportunity to help others by applying the tools I have developed, doing so with integrity, generosity, and honesty.

I hope my journey and the tools and tips presented in this book help you build your projects and your business, and becomes a shiny new addition to your own toolbox.

Michael Riegel
January 2020

CHAPTER 1

Is This Book For Me?

The landscape of public works construction is ever evolving, and many private companies are now beginning to take on the look and feel of a public agency, particularly from the perspective of supplier diversity and inclusion. In the industries I have worked in—construction, engineering, consulting, and utilities—there is increasing interest and pressure to provide opportunities for smaller companies that may not have the experience or financial resources to pursue major projects.

In many public agencies, small or medium-sized projects can be valued at $10 million+, far beyond the reach of many small businesses. The sheer size of the projects put them out of the reach of growing and emerging companies. However, public agencies as well as local, state and federal policy makers have made a concerted effort to promote the benefits of greater diversity. As a result, the implementation of diversity goals provides opportunities for companies that would ordinarily be shut out of real opportunities for growth. So, if you are reading this and realize you routinely interact with larger contractors, builders, or designers, there is something in here for you. If you are trying to figure out what tools you need to promote and foster the growth of your company, this book will provide you with practical tools and tips to help you achieve your goals. If you are trying to figure out ways to tighten up your operation or interact with clients more efficiently, they are in here. We have all heard the adage "work smarter, not harder"; this book will help you learn how to do just that without having to make all the mistakes first.

Why Did You Start A Business And Become A Small Business Owner?

This is a central question I ask my clients, and they often don't have a clear answer. For some, they were working for someone else, and after hearing enough times that all their hard work was putting profits in someone else's pocket, they decided to hang their own shingle and be the boss. For others, the business was inherited from a parent or other relative, whether or not the recipient actually had the background or technical expertise required to take over the business. There are dozens of reasons why people become entrepreneurs in the construction industry. If you are one of those entrepreneurs, I encourage you to really think about what it was that sparked your passion to be a business owner. Why? Because owning a business is not easy.

Too often, people are encouraged to start a business by friends or colleagues who may not really understand what it takes to succeed in our industry, or any industry. We would all appreciate a little less BS and a little more honesty—someone willing to put an arm around your shoulder and whisper the truth in your ear. The feeling I hope you get from reading this book is that of a reassuring *and* honest arm falling across your shoulder, and that you hear the truth about your business and the tools you will need.

The first bit of straight talk is that owning a business is harder and more complex than you imagined. The second is that it's not for people who are apathetic, inattentive, or lazy. The third is that, as a small business owner, your personal and professional lives are inextricably linked. It's like one of those novelty shop gifts where the more you try to untie the knot, the tighter it becomes someplace else. Separating the personal and professional is virtually impossible. This gets to the heart of creating some balance in your life. Small business owners never run out of things to do in the business and, without boundaries, it can take over your life, your family, and any kind of free time. The personal qualities that led you to start a business can also create tunnel vision and a loss of overall perspective.

For a while, you will be the proverbial chief cook and bottle washer, taking care of everything from writing proposals and creating estimates and schedules to preparing payrolls and regular bookkeeping, ordering supplies, and supervising staff, consultants, and field crews. Sounds like a lot of fun, right? As an emerging or growing enterprise, you may not have the latitude yet to bring in professionals to help run your business, so the best you can do is keep as many of the balls in the air as is humanly possible while you figure out some down time to recharge your batteries. As Jack Nicholson's character Jack Torrance famously typed over and over and over again in *The Shining*, "All work and no play makes Jack a dull boy." Working yourself to the point of exhaustion or frustration will not be good for you, your company, your employees, your clients, your family, your friends, or your projects.

This book is filled with stories, examples, quotes, and straight talk about how to manage your business and your life that others may not be willing to tell you directly.

Work On Your Business, Not In Your Business

My clients often tell me that, as owners, they feel they have to be involved all day, every day in every activity. This is frequently called "getting in the weeds" and the danger of getting too far into the weeds is that you can lose perspective and awareness of where you are headed. It is important to recognize when that perspective is getting a little fuzzy and you may be focusing on the individual tree instead of the forest. I subscribe to the theory that it is important to distinguish between *need to haves* and *nice to haves*. Essentially, prioritize activities and address the most pressing first, or sometimes the least challenging, to just get it done and out of the way. Throughout this book, I talk about the team of professionals you need around you to be successful, whether you are a specialty contractor, aspiring general contractor, construction manager, or trade contractor. Let me give you an example.

Jane owns a masonry and concrete company and works primarily with public agencies. Her firm does high-quality work and frequently performs as a subcontractor, helping meet compliance goals for various projects. Her firm is a certified woman-owned business (WBE is the certification designation and stands for Woman Business Enterprise) and is highly sought after by her clients. She has a project for which she is having difficulty getting paid in a timely manner. When I dug into the situation with her, she shared

that she signed her contract without a lawyer's review, and the payment terms were advantageous to the prime contractor—with no guarantees for her. She had a lawyer help her incorporate her business, but she did not see the value in spending $1,000 for a review of a contract that would yield over $100,000 in profit.

Jane took a position that was "penny wise but pound foolish." In other words, she opted for small savings at the risk of bigger costs. There can be a tendency to trust the client who wants to give you work and an excitement to start a new project—and those two factors, among many, can be problematic. I could appreciate her frugality. She didn't want to spend money on a lawyer that could detract from the overall profits. But from a big picture perspective, consulting with a lawyer might have fixed some of the payment issues she later encountered. From a support team perspective, key team members include an attorney, accountant, insurance agent, bonding agent, and financial planner to help you meet your future retirement goals. (Many forget about the financial planner, but as I described above, the intertwined nature of personal and professional lives makes a financial planner a key resource.)

At a gross level, small-business owners feel compelled to both work *in* and *on* their business, and the natural inclination is to focus on the former instead of the latter. What I hear is that working *on* the business feels like an afterthought or a luxury because it often does not involve doing a task with a tangible result. However, it's the strategic thinking of working *on* your business that allows you to sct goals, assess your strengths and weaknesses, and evaluate your current growth path. It is easy to be drawn to the working *in* the business side of the equation because it deals with the immediacies—putting out the fires—and generally can be measured in tasks completed. If you think about it as a balancing act, you may find you dedicate 80 percent of your time to working *in* and 20 percent working *on* your business, but I can't stress enough the importance of striking the right balance to get your business where you want and need it to be for long-term success and sustainability. The owner has to focus on growing the base of the business, identifying opportunities, profitability, and presenting the company in the best possible light.

I know what you're thinking...I can't afford all of that. In the beginning, that may be the case, but there are some absolutes you can't shortchange. It is imperative to have contracts reviewed and taxes and financial statements prepared professionally, and ensure you are covered appropriately from an insurance and bonding perspective. These are the basics you *must* find the money to cover. I have seen many contractors driving around in Mercedes Benz 500 Series cars (paid for by the business, of course) who cry poverty when it comes to covering the necessities for basic business health and growth. In the beginning, my advice is to forego luxury items and allocate resources to the business basics to protect and foster growth.

I am a huge fan of the TV show *The Profit*, where host Marcus Lemonis invests his own money in businesses where he sees potential for growth, and the need for structure, focus, and organization. No matter the potential business he is evaluating, he comes back to the same simple premise of *people, process, and product* to assess the work needed to "rightsize" the organization. For him, rightsizing means the ability to generate a profit, but he also understands the profit does not always show up on day one. It can take some time for businesses to gain traction and realize the benefits of the systems he puts in place.

There is beauty in this simplicity and, like Lemonis, I have developed my own lens through which to evaluate a company. Think of it as an empty toolbox with six compartments waiting to be filled. Each compartment represents a different area of your business:

 Finance

 Business Operations

 Communications

 Branding

 Marketing/Business Development

 Human Resources

Can you be successful without "earning" each new set of tools to fill the compartment? Sure, but the acceleration and growth of your business will be greater when you find balance across all six areas. The goal is to be a sustaining, thriving, and profitable company while striking the proper balance of attention among the six areas. I had a summer job working for a contractor and can still remember the awkwardness of carrying a lopsided load of materials. By filling your toolbox thoughtfully and carefully, you will create the foundation you need to support your personal and professional success.

And here's something to keep in mind: Small businesses are no different than large businesses, except that big companies have the latitude to pay for their mistakes—literally; they have the financial capacity to cover unexpected costs. Small businesses are more akin to a circus performer, walking the tightrope without a net and with what often feels like a refrigerator on their backs—with no margin for error. So, in that vein, you as a small business owner need to adopt a 4x4 mindset. You need to be:

 Competent;

 Qualified;

 Responsive; and

 Responsible—and you must be all four all the time.

What do each of these look like in actuality? *Competent* means that you are skilled and have the necessary background and experience to complete a particular task or project. *Qualified* reflects your company's ability, structure, and capacity to execute successfully. *Responsiveness*, at its core, is the agility to juggle not only the project work but also the calls and requests you get from clients, partners, and government entities. Deadlines are important, as are returning emails and phone calls in a timely manner—sometimes the first company to respond is the one that gets the job. Last, *responsibility* is essentially operating in an honest and forthright manner. Responsible companies understand their limitations and do not oversell and underperform, but undersell and overperform.

With each set of tools you "earn," I encourage you to think about how you can achieve 4x4 performance, because the opportunities are nearly limitless and the businesses that adopt and live that philosophy will quickly become the cream of the crop. You will find yourself being more selective, more successful, and revising your business goals on a regular basis. This theme of 4x4 performance and each of the four elements will show up for each of the six tools and how they can be considered for each. But first, let's talk about Larry.

Larry is a general contractor who has been in business for a few years and primarily completes small residential projects and the occasional commercial renovation. He has a trade he and his crew perform, and he understands his company's limitations. While he struggles with finding the right balance, our conversations are almost entirely about strategy, growth, and structure. He may not dedicate a lot of his workday to working on the business, but he is an active and enthusiastic participant in the conversation and wants to do things the right way. In my roles as coach, mentor, and consultant, I helped him look beyond his current projects to envision what was possible for him. Perhaps his biggest aha! moment came when he recognized he had to trust others so that he could focus on the big picture, and planning for what could be would serve him better than just complaining about what is. In the ensuing months, Larry spent more time scanning the horizon for the right opportunities and empowered his project manager to handle the day-to-day project details. He has since landed his largest contract to date that will be the cornerstone for his company's success. While the next chapters of his book are still unwritten, I have confidence in the power of his pen and newfound outlook.

I am not an idealist in my expectations with what can be accomplished in the short term; I'm a realist. I recall a professor I had in business school who taught finance and economics. He would famously chide the class to not chase the "short money," (a focus on short term vs. long term benefits) which was likely a message you would get from your accountant or financial planner. If you chase the short money, the high will subside and you will likely slide back to your original position. The takeaway is to begin developing long-term relationships that will help you grow your business for years to come. That means finding the right professionals to work with; your brother-in-law may have gone to law school but unless he has in-depth knowledge about your industry, he probably is not your best legal counsel. Your team members must understand your goals and your industry, and preferably be interconnected, since the issues they address individually are not easily compartmentalized (think financial statements/taxes and bonding/insurance).

The last piece of your team is the community of companies in your chosen industry. The development of a robust network will prove invaluable. The ability and willingness to be generous seems lost in our current business environment, but I can tell you there is no shortage of work for good companies that deliver the 4x4 proposition—companies that are *competent, qualified, responsive*, and *responsible*. Your network should include complementary firms (if you provide demolition services, find a trucking company you trust), competitors, potential clients, and past clients. Remember,

I'm not an idealist, but I have found that most people are generous and want to help. However, it does require you to reach out and connect with them.

And as you're getting to know others in the business, it's equally important to get to know yourself even better: your strengths; your weaknesses; your challenges; your dilemmas; and your opportunities. Below are some questions to get you started on the journey of self- and business-awareness.

CORNERSTONE QUESTIONS TO SUPPORT YOUR SUCCESS

- What excited you about the construction industry and why did you start your business?

- How much time do you spend working "in" the business (delivering, projects, managing staff, ordering materials) vs. "on" the business (sales, marketing, networking, client relationship management)? What about that proportion of time is working for you? What would you like to shift going forward?

- How would you describe your work-life balance now? How would you like it to be six months from now? In five years?

CHAPTER 2

My Nomadic Career—Collecting Personal And Professional Tools

I was recently called a "professional nomad"—and I took it as a compliment. My career has not followed a traditional or straight path. That does not mean there has not been a theme or thread that has run through the last thirty years, but on the outside the stops along the way have not always seemed sequential.

Being a professional nomad can provide tremendous opportunities for growth. And along the way, I collected a wide range of experiences I use to help others manage projects in the construction industry, for the residential, commercial, industrial, and public works sectors. These are my tools, the tools I needed to understand the industry, identify areas of improvement and opportunities for growth, and be a small business owner. If you peek into the toolbox in the back of your truck or on the jobsite, you will likely see signs of use on the tools used every day to physically build. You may have your own story of seemingly wandering through the industry collecting physical and virtual tools. Here's the thing I have realized: once you acquire the tool, you get to keep it to build your future, but the catch is you have to use it. Make sure you're using your virtual set of tools almost as often as your hammer or screwdriver—your business will be better for it.

Before I get too much further, let me roll the calendar back to explain how I got to where I am today as a coach, consultant, mentor, and speaker, and the general themes that have popped up at nearly every stop along my career.

Graduating Into 1990s Economic Uncertainty

My timing has not always been ideal; I graduated from college and graduate school into the deep valleys of job growth and opportunity. I began my career in 1992, a year before the economy began its recovery, and took a temporary position at the New York City Department of Transportation (NYCDOT).

What did I know at that point about public agencies and transportation? Virtually nothing! However, there were some generous people at the department who recognized a graduate with a degree in construction management who was seemingly bright, energetic, and willing to listen and learn could be a good fit. So, I went to work for the department in the special events planning group.

As it turns out, NYCDOT owns the streets of New York City, and I do mean *owns*. Nothing happens on the streets without the permission of and coordination with the NYCDOT and, not surprisingly, there is a lot that happens over the course of a year on the pavement around the five boroughs. I spent about nine months working with various outside groups that needed the city's highways and byways to hold their events. By a fortunate turn of events, 1992 was pretty special year in New York. We celebrated the 500th anniversary of Columbus landing in America, the 1992 Democratic National Convention was held at Madison Square Garden, and Fred Lebow (the founder of the NYC Marathon) ran his first and only marathon since becoming the race director, along with the standard events like the Macy's Thanksgiving Day Parade, a variety of bike tours, triathlons, parades, street fairs, and presidential visits. I even had the chance to sit in on planning meetings for a proposed Grand Prix car race through lower Manhattan that would have used the World Trade Center as the primary location. (Unfortunately, that did not materialize, but it would have been exciting.)

By the time December rolled around, there was not much going on, so I was asked if I'd be interested in moving to the traffic engineering group responsible for approving new traffic signals. Who was I to argue with a new opportunity? Off I went to the borough of Queens, where I really began my education in the technical aspect of transportation. This role gave me the chance to understand interpersonal dynamics, how to interact with elected officials, and the nuances associated with leading without authority. Somehow, I was invested with significant responsibility—all that for a temporary employee getting paid twelve dollars per hour—and got union-affiliated city employees to complete their traffic studies without too much complaining. I lasted about eight months before I decided health insurance and a permanent position might be a good idea, and found a position with a small traffic engineering and planning company that was an MBE.

Up until that point, the term Minority Business Enterprise (MBE) meant absolutely nothing to me. Why would it have? All I knew was that this small but growing company I was joining had enthusiastic owners with an open-door policy and other young staff in the infancy of their careers. Coincidentally, I still remain in contact with many of the people I worked with there, and we frequently retell the stories of the wafting smell of fish on Fridays (the offices were above an Irish pub that had fish as the Friday special) and the odd projects we completed. My colleagues and I from those early days often joke when we get together that college graduates would likely not be given the tasks we readily accepted, but we got the benefit of learning at pavement level and the education was invaluable.

I learned several valuable lessons over the ensuing four years. Written and verbal communications were crucial, even for technical professionals. We routinely wrote sections of environmental impact statements and had to convey information properly, accurately, clearly, and concisely. Our boss was a stickler with a felt tip pen and I became a much better writer who was provided with opportunities to write sections of proposals for new and existing clients. Perhaps more importantly, I learned about workplace integrity and what was referred to as *The New York Times* rule. The guidance we worked by was not to do anything that, if printed on the front page of *The New York Times*, would bring personal or professional embarrassment to us as individuals or to the firm. As the saying (often attributed to Will Rogers) goes, "It takes a lifetime to build a good reputation, but you can lose it in a minute." These are just a few of the important life and professional lessons that have stuck with me.

But what about the firm's MBE status? I came to learn that, for most public contracts, there were contracting goals for minority- and women-owned businesses. How was I to know this would become an integral part of the work I would get involved with nearly twenty years in the future?

That MBE firm continued to grow, but after four years I was itching for something bigger—a bigger company, greater responsibilities, expanded clients—and made the transition to a national firm with a traffic engineering group that interacted with civil engineers, structural engineers, architects, bridge designers, and inspectors. To be honest, I knew very little beyond my small corner of the operation, but we had an office principal who took me under his wing and pushed me to interact with the other technical groups. As a result, I can now joke that I know enough engineering to get myself in trouble. I asked questions and really listened to the answers, so that I could be helpful, and grow my knowledge base— and career.

Amazingly, this was still at a time when computer drafting was not standard. I would routinely pick the brain of my office neighbor— an eighty-five-year-old civil engineer from Hungary with a thick accent and wicked sense of humor who had likely forgotten more about highway design than I would ever know—and he was happy to explain the hows and whys. All the while, I began to become involved in managing aspects of projects, people, and budgets.

I quickly realized I appreciated those aspects of the industry and company a whole lot more than the technical engineering. So, in the six years I spent with that firm, I got heavily involved with operating budgets, profitability, staffing, operations, and project management and also took, as Robert Frost called it, the road less traveled.

Back To School

While my colleagues were pursuing advanced degrees in civil engineering and preparing for the professional engineering exams, I decided an MBA sounded more interesting and better aligned with my career goals. The traditional route for technical professionals is to further pursue technical education as a means of advancing a career, whether that is to get licensed as a professional engineer or complete a master's degree in engineering. I started down the path of a master's in civil engineering and quickly decided it was not the route for me. The backtracking might have been a seminal decision for my career progression. While I was working in a technical field for a technical organization, what interested me more was the opportunity to get involved in the nontechnical ("soft skills") aspects of a technical industry, such as employee management and supervision, client relationship building, and strategic planning.

In the Zicklin MBA program at Baruch College, I felt like a fish out of water, but then I suppose that was likely a common feeling if you polled the twenty-four other students in our cohort.

We had three medical professionals, and people from the arts, nonprofits, and other nontraditional business types mixed with a few from banking and management consulting. The random mix of professions and personalities was a great living lab, and the most interesting course for me was Organizational Behavior. I was fascinated to learn the theory of what made organizations and employees function and react, and I got the chance to tinker at work to see what I wanted to adopt longer term.

Getting my graduate degree also provided a unique opportunity to hone my work-life balance skills: I was working full-time during the day, attending school on the weekends, while my wife Deborah was home on bedrest while pregnant with our twins—meaning all household chores were also my responsibility (and I do mean *all*). My toolbox was growing by the day and my goal was to find a place to scuff up the tools, and to use them in a new and novel way.

On The Caravan Again

After six years and a completed MBA (and now a set of twins at home), my professional caravan left for a two-year stint at a consulting engineering firm before I landed at a regional utility company.

There are times when you look back, and despite the stress and strife of a job, realize the experience provided so many opportunities for growth that you can only smile and appreciate it with the passage of

ROUTE TO THE TOP

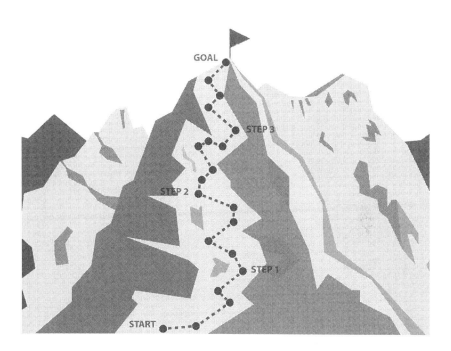

time. This is one of those times. I was brought in at a time when the gas company was implementing a resource management strategy for the first time and had worked with a Big Four accounting firm to lay out the basics of the program. As I quickly came to learn, the consultants were much more interested in structuring the program from a view at 50,000 feet and were not nearly as focused on the actual day-to-day challenges of implementing it within the existing organizational structure.

I also came to understand that, in many ways, utilities have not changed much with respect to business models and structure in decades, so trying a new and radically different approach upset a few people. We also had to implement the new approach to capital construction in a management-labor environment that required holding crews accountable for productivity—no easy task. I was considered a perfect candidate for this new position for a number of reasons: I had a background in engineering and construction; I had an MBA and a more broad-based perspective; and I was not part of the organization, and therefore somewhat insulated from the concept of "we've always done it that way."

I was the new guy when I joined the company, and five years later, I was still the new guy. The turnover was remarkably low, which corralled a lot of institutional knowledge, but which also crowded out new ideas and approaches when it came to resource management.

The Basics Of Resource Management

What is resource management? Essentially, it is a structured and enhanced planning function that takes into account costs, schedules, work crews, productivity, and outside contractors. I frequently say I lived in three time frames at once—the past, present, and future. I had to understand past performance and the root causes for schedule and cost performance (positive and negative) with an eye to ensuring the things done well were acknowledged and brought forward, and what did not go well was noted so we could avoid the problems in the future.

The present situation included the current work year and, more prominently, the implementation of a two- to eight-week look ahead to identify challenges to productivity, completion of projects, and the need for outside contractor crews to help meet annual targets. At the same time, I had to keep an eye on the following program year, the impacts of external projects, changes in regulations, adjustments in corporate goals, and a projection of annual expenditures. It was not easy living in all those time frames or assuaging the labor unions that viewed our enhanced planning activities as a criticism of their level of effort.

My wife Deborah often joked about whether I should have someone else start my car at the end of the day—I believe she may have seen one too many mob movies—but in truth, I was not considered an ally of union leadership. There were some key takeaways from my time at the utility company: a great boss can make all the difference in the world, working through adversarial situations can yield consensus, it is sometimes better to plead ignorance and listen for an explanation, and old dogs can learn some new tricks.

I remain in close contact with my boss/colleague/friend and we frequently catch up over lunch or drinks to discuss our professional challenges and have a few laughs about our shared experiences and how they remain instructive, useful, and sometimes mind-boggling.

I often tell younger staff that when you find a good supervisor, your job becomes infinitely easier because you are given autonomy, authority, permission to develop creative approaches, and the latitude to make mistakes. I was fortunate to find those qualities at a position that proved pivotal to my personal and professional development. By the time five years had quickly rolled by, I began receiving calls from recruiters—perhaps my timing was not always bad—as the crash of 2008 had turned into a slow recovery by mid-2010. Looking back on it, my toolbox was definitely filling up and the tools inside were getting good use and showing signs of wear.

Another Stop Along The Way

I was not looking to make a lateral move again as I had with the utility company, so I was selective about what I would consider. When a national engineering and construction management (CM) firm was looking for a program manager to handle its entire New York CM portfolio, my ears perked up. I kept thinking, "this is a new experience" and the opportunities for growth seemed limitless. For the first time, I would have the responsibility of managing client relationships, hiring and supervising staff, and tracking and controlling performance of various contracts—and the job came with a closed-door office! The last one was really just the cherry on top of the sundae, although the changing nature of office environments now makes that a serious perk. At the time, we had over $2 billion in active construction throughout New York and nearly $25 million in annual fees to manage it.

As I had found in previous caravan stops, there was a lot to learn about this facet of the industry and I leaned heavily on my natural curiosity and willingness to get out in the field and ask questions. Adages can often seem trite, but when appropriately applied can be very powerful. "You were given two ears and one mouth; listen twice as much as you speak" is a simple message that has traveled with me throughout the learning process. I also found getting out to project sites gave me insight into what some of the problems were and could be in the future. I learned this from counting cars (literally) as a young traffic engineer and observing utility construction crews. I would routinely visit the projects and ask for a tour of the site, which was typically met with "but your pants and shoes will get dirty." Inspectors were surprised when my response was, "Yes, and the pants can go to the cleaners and the shoes can be shined."

Hip Deep In The You-Know-What With Them— Literally

The stories we retain are often instructive and funny although the true meaning does not reveal itself for some time. On one site visit of a wastewater treatment plant, an inspector advised me to hold my breath as we were entering a particular room. How long did he think I could hold my breath? Did I look like an Olympic swimmer? Well, inside the room was the top of a five-story cauldron of hot, brown, bubbling . . . well, crap. It was noxious and I held my breath for as long as possible. He could not have prepared me for just how vile it was, but he at least set some expectations of what I would experience.

Several months later, my company was alerted to a fire in the same plant that had damaged motors, preventing operations. Understand this plant processes about 140 million gallons of wastewater and sewage per day, and while it was offline, it got dumped directly into the Hudson River. Yes, that is bad, but the river could disperse it over time. The bigger challenge was the impact on water quality, as the NYC Triathlon was planned for three weeks later, and yes, they swim in the Hudson River.

Working around the clock with many of the other CM firms, the plant was brought online in time for the race. That is secondary to my experience working twelve-hour shifts overnight in the August heat and humidity with our inspectors to make repairs. One evening, a colleague named Jim said to me, "What the hell are you doing here? You went to college so you wouldn't have to do this." My response has been a personal philosophy for as long as I can recall: "I can't ask you to do something I'm not willing to do." Consequently, I have found staff willing to do things they might not prefer because they have always seen my willingness to roll up my sleeves, get my hands and pants dirty, and help out when needed. This was another work-life lesson I could pack into my toolbox.

Those Who Can, Teach

Unfortunately, my professional caravan got derailed by a corporate restructuring that left me on the outside looking in, and I spent the ensuing four years taking contract assignments with nonprofits, public agencies, and private schools, providing project management, data analysis, operational support, and process reengineering services. Remembering the need for continuous improvement, in skills and knowledge, I used the hiatus from full-time employment to go back to school to become a coach. Not a coach in the sense of my kid's little league team, but an executive, management, and career coach. This new professional step was a natural fit for my interest, willingness, and skill in supervising staff and helping them envision solutions, and selecting the most promising path forward for their personal and professional goals.

Many do not understand the true nature of coaching—they think of it as telling, advising, or fixing; however, much of coaching comes down to active listening, asking powerful questions, and holding clients accountable for their decisions. Without even knowing it, I was dropping in a whole different set of tools into my toolbox—tools and skills to be learned, practiced, used, and perhaps never perfected but honed and sharpened. These skills, in addition to those in my now-burgeoning toolbox, came in very handy by the time I decided I wanted to return to an organizational role I never could have envisioned or anticipated. The first of real interest was from a firm that had a contract to manage a construction mentoring program for a regional transportation agency—back to public sector clients in a particular area of expertise: construction management. While that role did not work out, a year later the company was awarded a contract with the same client to provide technical assistance and training to the contractors in the mentor program and they reached out to see if I might be interested and available.

 They needed someone who could develop and implement the program. *Check.*

 They needed someone who understood public agencies and general procurement. *Check.*

 They needed someone to build and supervise a staff. *Check.*

 They wanted someone who understood training and could evaluate the current program. *Check.*

 They needed someone who could effectively interact with the contractors, agency staff, and outside consultants. *Check.*

 They needed someone who was willing and able to represent the program, recruit participants, and explain the benefits of the program to other agencies. *Check.*

It seemed as though I was checking off all their boxes, and at the same time, it was a chance to manage a program that intrigued me. I had no idea at the time how much I would come to learn and the myriad contacts I would develop along the way.

For the following two years, I worked tirelessly to build a staff and figure out how to implement a scope of work (not necessarily exactly as it was written), but most importantly, I had the opportunity to work with many, many, many small business owners. I would often describe my philosophy as it related to our construction contractors like this: "I will no longer call you a contractor; you are a small business owner. You have employees, you have to make payroll, and you have to worry about profitability. If I call you a contractor, then I have lowered the bar to the point where I could trip over it." While the program was not specifically designed for MBEs, WBEs, and SDVOBs (service-disabled veteran-owned businesses), a preponderance of the companies in it were certified in one capacity or another. It seemed an apt bookend to my first job working as a traffic engineer for a certified MBE.

Certifications are a ripe target of conversation within the industry, and more and more states and local municipalities are assigning goals to public projects that acknowledge the historical disadvantages of these groups. If I am being 100 percent honest, my favorite part of the job was having a small business owner in a conference room where we could discuss business goals, challenges, opportunities, and solutions. It became the perfect mix of all I had done in my career for the purpose of helping small business owners grow their businesses in a reasonable and controlled manner. But (and there always seems to be a but) a word or two about certifications is needed. There are many who believe certification is some sort of guarantee or entitlement to securing work with an agency or prime contractor. In those conference rooms working with small business owners, I frequently found myself giving them straight talk. I would figuratively put my arm across their shoulders and whisper in their ears, "Your certification only unlocks the door. Now you have to go through the door, prove yourself, and provide value every day." That is a consistent message I deliver to any small business owner entering the industry who may have been told that somehow the certification is a golden ticket to success.

And so, that last experience rounded out thirty years working with public agencies in the execution of projects in the engineering and construction fields and gave me the opportunity to work with dynamic and enthusiastic small business owners. It further expanded my toolbox and gave me the push to pursue the opportunity to do that privately and write this book.

Do I know everything? Absolutely not. I consider myself a lifelong learner and sometimes the most important thing to know is what you *don't* know, but can learn where to find the information. As I said, the beauty of acquiring tools along your professional journey is they can't be taken away from you, and the toolbox always has room to expand. By using the tools often, they become sharper and more useful, and you, as the small business owner, become more accustomed and skilled in putting them into practice, making you more effective, efficient, and professional so you can operate just like the big primes in the industry.

CORNERSTONE QUESTIONS TO SUPPORT YOUR SUCCESS:

- What lessons have you learned throughout your career that have impacted you as a small business owner today?

- What experiences have you had that make you unique and relevant to your clients, teaming partners, and vendors?

- What general themes do you see across the span of your career, and how can you use them to your benefit and success?

- What is the story you tell yourself when reflecting on your career? How does this story serve you moving forward?

CHAPTER 3

The *Build Like The Big Primes* System: An Overview

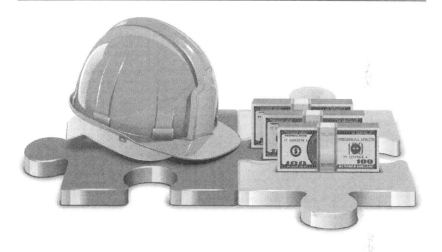

At a certain point, I started to experience the convergence of the different parts of my career and began to envision a way to help business owners articulate and achieve their business goals. In the same way as when I worked for the utility in Resource Management and things came into my head like puzzle pieces to be aligned in a particular sequence, I began to develop a system in a visual way to address all the components I had been thinking about.

The first image was of the game piece in Trivial Pursuit with six openings—each for a wedge in a different category. During the process of refining the system, the game piece was ultimately represented by the toolbox in my workshop with its compartments and trays—every tool in its place and a place for every tool. I began to recognize that there was significant applicability in what I experienced working for large firms and organizations to the community of small business owners I was working with, and that providing a structured system and roadmap would be useful for helping them be successful—in whatever capacity that looked like for them individually. My work with small and emerging companies in the construction industry helps them establish credibility with public agencies, prime contractors, and organizations that focus on increasing diversity and inclusion in the delivery of construction projects.

My clients primarily do work in the public sector as well as in the commercial and residential sectors, and they are amazing at what they do. But usually, their passion for their work is in delivering awesome projects; they need a bit of assistance with the *business of building and managing their businesses.* For many, the idea of managing and delivering projects seems like second nature; they learned by seeing and doing at the side of someone more experienced. The technical part of building a project can almost be seen in the calloused hands and heard in the war stories. However, from the perspective of building and managing a business, most of my clients did not have a role model or apprentice program to show them the ropes. As a business owner, the ability to build the projects and manage the business with equal levels of confidence and expertise is the "secret sauce" to long term success.

Throughout my professional career working in a variety of roles across industries, I learned invaluable lessons about the tools and skills required for a company's success. And these lessons are universal; they apply to small and medium-sized businesses as well as larger organizations that routinely hire subcontractors and subconsultants to help them provide services and guidance to the smaller firms.

A structured, systematic approach to mentoring emerging leaders in the construction sector is a passion for me. This system identifies many of the challenges faced by small companies that can't leverage or pursue larger contracts—yet.

The *Build Like The Big Primes* system is simple, but it is not easy. It requires self-discipline, attention, commitment, and the willingness to step outside established routines and comfort zones. It doesn't provide a missing puzzle piece where, once you find it, you can snap it into place and—voila!—your biggest business challenge is solved. It requires the inclination to learn and apply new skills, new strategies, new structures, and new philosophies. It may require releasing outdated or unproductive beliefs, methods, and systems. It requires experimentation, an openness to looking into the toolbox to see what you have, what you need, and what will put you on the path to growth and operating like the big players in the industry.

In the following chapters, we will explore the approach in detail, including stories about others who have taken the journey, filled their toolboxes, grown their own construction businesses, and found the success they wanted. Throughout the next chapters, your tools will be presented in a consistent theme I use almost universally in working with emerging contractors that aspire to build like the big primes: the concept of 4x4 performance, which I briefly mentioned in chapter 1.

In some companies, 4x4 performance is considered to be on time, on budget, safely, and with a satisfied client. Those things are all important for a construction contractor, but for aspiring and emerging contractors (particularly certified contractors), the 4x4 perspective used throughout this book is *competent, qualified, responsive, and responsible.* This does not mean that the "traditional" view of 4x4 performance is not important to keep in mind as it relates to the delivery of projects but that this perspective on 4x4 performance is directly applicable to the management of your business. This view is more expansive than that related to projects and they can and should coexist in order to accelerate and maintain your personal and business growth.

This is the price of admission to a bigger game and you don't really have the latitude to pick and choose. Consistent 4x4 performance is needed if you want to build like the big companies.

In this book, you will also find usable and practical tips associated with each set of tools you can implement in your business and try out for yourself. These are all tips you can customize for your company and experiment with to make them feel right for your personality and way of doing business.

One important note: It doesn't matter how successful your business is if you don't operate with integrity. Integrity is defined as "the quality of being honest and having strong moral principles; moral uprightness." We all have stories about or experiences with dishonest or disreputable contractors. In many respects, that is one of the stereotypes of contractors we try to dispel or avoid as much as possible. "Say what you mean and mean what you say" is a quote that has been attributed to many, including Dr. Seuss and General George Patton. The true origin may be unknown, but the idea is powerful in and of itself. It goes directly to the heart of integrity, standing by your word, and delivering on promises. The big companies did not (or will not) succeed long term and grow by cutting corners, cheating, dealing from the bottom of the deck, or whatever metaphor resonates with you. If you aspire to be like the big primes (even if you prefer to remain in your niche), it is advisable to adopt their ethics and philosophies. Say what you mean and mean what you say!

The *Build Like The Big Primes* Toolbox

Tools come in all shapes and sizes and categories. In your local Home Depot or Lowes, they are typically arranged so you can easily find what you are looking for—electrical, plumbing, lighting, flooring, etc. The business tools we are talking about are arranged similarly and are grouped into six categories—Finance, Operations, Communications, Personal Branding, Marketing, and Human Resources. So, whatever you are shopping for can be easily found and put to use in building your business.

 Your Finance Tools. You are in business to make money; that is the essential purpose of a business. The finance tools are key to understanding profitability, goals, and capacity. Growth will be fostered or restricted by your business's financial position, as well as your knowledge and ability to discuss finances confidently and competently. Perhaps the most critical of all the tools you can secure in your toolbox, these skills will enable you to know your numbers, talk about your numbers (and tell the right story), and break it all down (get to the details so you can plan for future growth). The goal is not to transform you from contractor to accountant, but to give you an awareness of the importance of paying attention to your company and project finances, reviewing your financial statements on a regular basis, and the need to build out your finance team. The last thing you want to hear is that an opportunity is beyond your reach because you have not ensured your finances are solid, are secure, and inspire confidence.

 Your Operations Tools. When we think about the operations and administration of businesses, we must consider the processes and procedures that ensure the smooth and efficient management of the overall business. While many may not consider operations tools to be vital to the business, think about what would happen if there were no structure or support for the delivery of projects. In addition to developing your team of professionals to support your growth (attorneys, accountants, bonding and insurance agents, bankers), the operations tools ensure you can complete a project, bill and collect your fees, align your business and plan for future growth, and operate safely. Key to transforming your role from contractor to business owner, these tools help inform the status of your business and manage it in a comprehensive manner. As a business owner, you can't possibly do it all yourself; the acquisition and implementation of operations tools will allow you to do more, know more, and grow more.

 Your Communications Tools. Are there really any elements of managing your business, delivering projects, or winning additional work that do not rest on the ability to communicate? And not just communicate, but to do so clearly, concisely, and effectively? Some might say the communications tools you develop and use are the foundation for all the other tools, whether that is in finance, operations, marketing, branding, or human resources. The trick to communications is in tailoring your means and methods to the recipient of the message being delivered. In financial matters, it is not just the actual numbers, but also the story you want to tell about the growth and health of your business. Functionally and practically, communications may focus on industry professionals or service providers and you need to ensure they have confidence in you and understand your overall needs. Effective communications are integral to the marketing and branding efforts of your business—ensuring potential clients clearly understand what you do and your value proposition. Finally, without communications, you will encounter challenges hiring and retaining staff as well as setting clear expectations and assessing performance. In any one of these areas, it is critically important to consider what message you want to deliver, your language choice and how it may be received, and the implications of getting it wrong. Perhaps the most important aspect of communications can be boiled down to one axiom you've already heard from me: Say what you mean and mean what you say.

 Your Personal Branding Tools. As a small business owner, you are the public face of your company, whether your face (and the rest of you) is at an industry event on a Thursday night, at the local supermarket on a Saturday morning, or posting on Facebook on Sunday night. This is important, because the way you carry and present yourself everywhere will be a reflection on the company in the eyes of your clients, agencies, suppliers, and employees—both current *and* prospective. What reputation do you want to develop for yourself as a leader and for your company? Branding starts by setting a good example for your employees—showing up on time and properly equipped—and displaying professionalism no matter where you are.

My wife Deborah was a competitive public speaker in high school (yes, that's a real extracurricular activity), and she learned as a teenager that anybody could be your judge: The people she saw in the elevator at the headquarters hotel or the group standing in line behind her at the breakfast buffet could be her judges in the tournament later that day. As a result, she knew that every behavior can be noticed, and that every behavior counts. (She eventually won the national championship, so she must have been doing something right!)

When we think about the branding tools you will put into your toolbox, it is important to realize these might actually be the ones that get the most frequent use, since they will come out every time you have a meeting, go to a jobsite, attend a conference, or call a client.

An advertisement from the 1960s by Botany Suits used the tagline, "You never get a second chance to make a first impression." This is a core part of your personal and professional branding, except once you make a good first impression, you and your team have to maintain it.

Your Marketing Tools. Many companies think marketing tools are strictly about waiting for emails to come in and submitting estimates as a result of the company's certification. I have heard, too many times to count, that the industry is just based on dollars and cents, so there is no need to pick up the phone, meet a potential client, or attend an industry event. Invariably, companies and agencies like to work with businesses they know and trust. Your marketing tools will help you grow your business by being clear about the kind of work you do well, the type of work you should be focusing on, and the companies or agencies that are "buying what you are selling." This also includes being clear about what you *don't* do, and being a helpful, generous, and honest referral source for other businesses who do related work. Your marketing toolbox needs to also be stocked with materials you can send to potential clients that present your business in the best possible way. These tools will include your business card, capability statement, and website address. Your marketing efforts should make it easy for your target clients to say "yes," which means providing them with your corporate information, including your certifications, safety records, and commodity codes.

Your Human Resources Tools. Where would your business be without the labor or human resources necessary to build the projects you are winning through your newly acquired marketing tools? What will happen if you don't hire the right people, or fail to manage your employees effectively and proactively? Hiring and retaining employees can be a challenge for growing businesses, but through thoughtful engagement, you can build a loyal team that will represent you appropriately and happily respond to your requests. And it's not just about the money. The HR tools are going to get used from the moment you realize you need additional staff until you decide you are getting out of the business. These tools will include job applications, policies and procedures, and benefit packages (all tangible items), as well as performance reviews, training, and motivation.

Managing people, all with different personalities, perspectives, and needs, is a skill that many small business owners can recognize, but have not had the need to hone. Using the HR tools often and getting comfortable in this area of the business will set you apart from your competitors and make it easier to grow and potentially make the transition to union affiliation, if that is the path you choose. Finally, the two most valuable sets of tools I gathered on my nomadic journey—and have been able to keep in my personal toolbox through the value of lifelong learning—were related to coaching and mentoring. Coaching and mentoring tools are the advanced tools that have helped set the foundation of my own success, and will help distinguish you from your peers as a business owner, trusted advisor, and valued partner. They will also open the possibility that you may need an empty toolbox for a brand new set of tools!

CORNERSTONE QUESTIONS TO SUPPORT YOUR SUCCESS:

- Which of the six tools (finance, operations, communications, branding, marketing, and human resources) feel more developed than others?

- Which tools feel less developed?

- Which tools would you prioritize to generate the greatest benefit?

- Which tools do you notice yourself avoiding or minimizing? How might you shift your perspective or attitude to embrace those tools?

CHAPTER 4

Your Finance Tools: Making Money Is Only The Start

For many, finance is a subject that is avoided like the plague. I am often taken aback when I talk to contractors and potential clients and observe how much they do not want to talk about money and company finances, whether out of embarrassment (not earning enough), discomfort (insufficient tracking systems), or shame (not turning a profit). We all seem to be hardwired to shun discussing money among colleagues. Can you recall a time when coworkers were transparent about their salaries? Neither can I. We live in fear that there will be judgment associated with whatever the numbers are, but as a business owner, this is a topic you need to become comfortable with. No, I am not advocating you act like an extra in a commercial for financial planning companies where people walk around with signs around their necks identifying their net worth. However, becoming more comfortable discussing the financial health, growth, and sustainability of your business will be enlightening and freeing—if you find the right team to support you.

This chapter will introduce you to some concepts that will promote business and personal growth and help develop your financial acumen. The focus is on two concepts: acquiring the financial tools for your toolbox that will help you meet your goals (whatever they are) and modeling the way big primes operate even if you don't aspire to be that big. After all, your company can achieve both by using enhanced tools and working smarter, not harder.

Know Your Numbers

Here's a client example:

John has been in business for several years, but complained that his company was not growing the way he wanted it to, even though he was getting a lot of work as a subcontractor. One of the first questions I asked him was, "What was your revenue last year, and what do you expect it to be this year?" His response, after a very long pause, was: "Um . . . I'm not really sure." Without judging him for not knowing the answer, I asked him to print out his profit and loss statement for the current and past year. As it turned out, John was up-to-date on his bookkeeping and had the information at his disposal. He just needed to review it more often. Knowledge is power, but information is not knowledge. John had information but, because he was not reviewing it, he was not generating the knowledge he actually needed.

Compare and contrast that with another client: Beth's construction business had consistent growth over the last five years when she came to me to help her accelerate it and meet her financial goals. I asked Beth the same series of questions I had asked John. She was able to tell me off the top of her head that she had grown from $500,000 in revenue to $3 million in the five-year period. After congratulating her on that achievement, I asked her, "How big do you want to get and over what period of time?" Proudly, she told me that in the next five years she wanted to bring in $20 million in *revenue. Beth has managed tremendous growth and was hoping to continue on a very steep growth curve.*

I remember before we all had GPS built into our phones or our cars, we had to rely on maps—yes, those foldout maps that never wanted to go back to their original state. The beauty of those maps was that you could plot and track your course from where you started to your final destination and seeing all of the points in between. Our current GPS also gets you to your final destination, but the view on the screen is very limited. Your financial statements—beyond the profit and loss—provide you with the old-school view of your company's progress toward your destination. Without knowing what you have achieved in the past, it is difficult to establish future goals, assess profitability, determine potential challenges, and think about your personal and corporate capacity for more work. Knowing your numbers is critical to goal setting and measuring your performance against your planned achievements.

I know there are books that are dedicated to company finances and accounting, and I'm also pretty sure I have one or two of those books on my shelf. They can be very informative, but often neglect the fact that emerging companies do not have payroll departments, accounting staff, and teams of analysts like larger companies. So, what's a small company to do? Your finances are a direct result of the work you are bidding, delivering, completing, and closing out. Your ability to develop transparency around this process will help you gain a better understanding of your projected cash flow, along with your ability to meet your commitments and take on larger projects. I universally encourage my clients—and any business owner I talk to—to develop some structure for themselves that can help them track projects from the sales process through to completion. The caveat I always offer is to include not only the value of the project, but also the expected gross profit. Of course, gross profit is not the same as net profit, and I caution companies to include an appropriate profit margin in their bids. When I teach classes to companies in the construction industry, I like to put up the following equation to illustrate this point:

---

10 = 0
A gross profit of 10 percent generally will erode to near 0 percent for many reasons.

Your Numbers Tell A Story

Among the documents I ask a new client to have on hand when we meet for the first time—yes, first time—are the company financial statements for at least the last two full years and for the current year to date. Why? Because the statements tell a story about the health, efficiency, and growth potential of the company. This includes:

 Balance sheet

 Profit and loss or income statement

 Cash flow statement

 Work in progress schedule

 Completed projects schedule

These are important tools for a business owner and tell a story about the company, the owner as a businessperson, the ability to pursue bigger work, and the owner's readiness to take the next step. So, what story do they tell?

My client Jim has been in business for many years with some good years and some not as good. That is not surprising, as most businesses have to deal with the general ups and downs of the economy at large. As I reviewed his statements, I began asking questions about particular expenses that seemed out of the ordinary: minimal personal payroll and tax expenses. He sheepishly admitted he basically takes what is left at the end of the year as his salary. For Jim, the story was about not managing his cash flow to ensure he could take a regular salary, which was further indication he was not tracking his projects financially with any real level of specificity.

The story your statements tell might be something totally different, but be aware that the ability to tell a good story—without fudging—is critical when it comes to meeting with your bonding agent to secure or increase your surety bonding capacity. At the end of the day, a surety bond is no different than an insurance policy for your client, and I can guarantee your bonding agent will pore over your financials with a lot more scrutiny than I would. So, the story you want to tell is one of financial health, stability, and responsibility. Where do things go off the rails? A few examples:

 Judgments against the company and business owner for failure to pay taxes (personal, corporate, payroll, etc.)

Liens for failure to complete projects and exercising your performance bond

 Previous assessment of liquidated damages

All this information becomes part of the public record, so take care to ensure you present the best story possible. Remember *The New York Times* rule? Don't do something you would not want published on its front page. This concept applies to your personal and corporate finances as well. Don't do things with your finances that, were they made public, would make you feel embarrassed, ashamed, or require some serious explaining. The companion thought is that it takes a long time to build a reputation that can be destroyed with a single act. Don't assume you can cut corners and nobody will be the wiser—someone always finds out.

Once you know and are comfortable talking about your numbers and have a good idea of what story they tell the outside world, what else do you need to be mindful of? Well, uncontrolled or aggressive growth without the infrastructure to support new revenue levels can be even more risky and potentially disastrous than not realizing the growth you might desire. With growth comes a lot more expense and challenges—new equipment, more staff, increased insurance and bonding, and the need to sustain increased revenue levels. Unless you have the skill and will to fully manage the money appropriately, which includes engaging the right professionals, the likelihood of long-term success will be diminished, and you hold the professional and financial well-being of your employees in your hands. Remember Beth, whose goal was to grow so rapidly? For business owners like her, I offer that the real trick is not developing a $20 million revenue stream for a single year, but sustaining that year after year. Achieving $20 million in revenue for one year does not make it a $20 million business, at least not until that target is hit for a sustained period.

Break It All Down

When I was a child, my parents would stress the importance of estimating (not in the sense of work hours or project costs) and the ability to do mental math. Mental math is not about being a human calculator and getting to an exact answer (which my daughter Sophie can actually do), but the ability to get close enough so you can make reasoned choices. Having grown up in a family with two parents who were New York City public school teachers, those estimating skills became central to determining whether a vacation or purchase was feasible on teachers' salaries. As a small business owner, I find these skills valuable for me as I assess the company's financial ability in round numbers. I like to couple this approach with the idea of working in round numbers that can be easily digested. When I work with clients on their planned growth and desired revenue, I make sure we break it down into more digestible bites. Beth, who wanted to create a $20 million annual revenue stream, picked a number out of thin air, one that is a challenge to conceptualize. I said, "How about we work with $18 million for planning purposes?" Why $18 million? It breaks down easily over the span of twelve months—$1.5 million per month. Further, it breaks down to $750K every two weeks, which matches up with her standard payroll periods. Here's a tip: Don't get too hung up on the details—I know some months have five weeks and three pay periods—but we are just talking about high-level planning. Here is where your knowledge of your financial situation becomes critical.

What does it cost you on average for each of your employees? Not what you pay them, but total cost, which includes administration, overhead, equipment cost, professional services, owner salary, taxes, insurance, rent, bonding, *and* profit. If we are considering $1.5 million per month as your top line number, we need to build the hourly rate for your employees to include all the items that will hit the top line or gross revenue. The likelihood is if you are paying an employee $50 per hour, the fully loaded rate for that person will be $100 per hour or more. Let's use $150 per hour as our planning rate. How many employee hours does your staff as a whole have to work at $150 per hour to bank $750K per pay period? That's 5,000 hours every two weeks, 2,500 hours every week, and working eight hours per day, it tips the scale at a little more than 300 person-days per week. If you are working your projects five days per week—hopefully—you will need about sixty full-time employees to meet your revenue goal.

We are talking about planning, right? We know the workload is not a straight line from January to December; it is likely to be bell-shaped with less work from the beginning of November to the end of February, depending on the type of work you perform. Even if you provide design services, clients tend to get very quiet from the middle of November through early January with holidays and vacations. All this means the middle eight months will need to exceed those planning levels to cover for the months that will invariably fall short. Is there more to be considered in this process? Definitely.

I am a planner (by nature) and project manager (by profession), so I like to work the process forward and backward—similar to a Critical Path Method (CPM) schedule. (This is the place in my discussions with my wife Deborah where I can see her eyes glaze over as she slowly starts to back out of the room.) There are other elements to be considered besides the finances that are discussed later in the book, but this process gives you an idea about how realistic your goals are. If you have a solid crew of ten that is working all year long, that gives you a base of about $3 million in gross revenue per year, based on our model numbers.

As I go through this exercise with clients and we discuss current projects, signed contracts for upcoming work, and projects they are pursuing, it becomes clearer as to what is possible and what is probable. Planning for growth and having growth targets are great, but I encourage you to make sure they are reasonable and achievable, and you have a good sense of the implications of meeting those goals. It's sometimes helpful to think about the dog that chases the car and one day catches it—the dog never really ever had an expectation of catching the car and has no idea what to do when he manages to latch on to the bumper.

Here are some critical elements when it comes to company finances to keep in mind:

 Develop your finance team—accountant for taxes, bookkeeping, insurance agent, bonding agent, personal financial planner.

 Track your individual projects based on planned and actual profit.

 Forecast cash flow for each project.

 Keep the cash in the business—*cash is king!*

 Avoid unnecessary expenses.

If You Can Measure It, You Can Manage It

By knowing, tracking, and getting comfortable with the financial aspect of your business, you can think about taking it to the next level of projecting, planning, and preparing for growth. Be willing to pull the virtual tape measure from your toolbox so you can, on a regular basis, measure how far you have come and how much further you need to go to meet your goals. In the beginning, you may focus on the core financial aspects of your business, but as you get more comfortable and skilled at asking the right questions, the measuring tool will become more detailed and sophisticated. This will allow you to dig deeper into your business's finances and make better decisions about opportunities, growth, profit, and expenses.

When you think about growing your business and building like the big primes, it is important to remember they became big players in the market because they understood their numbers—from estimating and expenses to revenue projections and backlog—and used them to effectively make decisions. In the beginning, focus on the most critical aspect of your business and as you grow, you will have the opportunity to begin examining your financial metrics like the big players in the industry.

4X4 IN FINANCE

How can you deliver 4x4 performance as it relates to your finances?

 Financial *competence* is evidenced by a solid understanding of your financial position, regular updates and current bookkeeping, ongoing discussions with your accountant, and satisfying your financial commitments (i.e., vendors, subcontractors, suppliers, tax entities, partners, etc.).

 Are you *qualified* to execute the vision and size of the projects you are pursuing? This will involve the development of a relationship with a bank or lending institution before you need to borrow money, as well as a relationship with a bonding agent. Coupling your competence and qualification will put you in an advantageous position to capitalize on opportunities as they arise.

 Your *responsiveness* to requests for financial information (e.g., from a bank, prime contractor, government entity, or client) delivers a sense of confidence in you as a business owner as well as your company's ability to execute financially.

 Fiscal and financial *responsibility* can be measured in many ways. Clients entertaining a contract in excess of your prior project sizes will look to your payment history on previous loans, outstanding credit lines, or whether you are overextended, limiting your ability to secure additional financing.

These all point to your ability to demonstrate good financial stewardship of your own business and instill confidence in potential clients that you will be a good steward of their money, and thereby reduce their financial risk.

CORNERSTONE QUESTIONS TO SUPPORT YOUR SUCCESS:

- How has your upbringing or childhood impacted your overall relationship with money and finance? What would you like to preserve or change about your financial history?

- What story do your financial statements tell you? What story would they convey to your clients or banking partners? What story do you want them to tell?

- What opportunities might open up for you if you felt more comfortable discussing your finances?

- Where can you start to experiment (even in a small way) with talking about money with greater comfort and frequency?

CHAPTER 5

Your Operations Tools: The Nuts And Bolts Of Running The Business

In my work with small business owners, an area of common concern and challenge is operations—concern they are not properly managing their business and challenge because they often do not strike a balance between working *in* and *on* the business.

The reality is that emulating the big primes at this stage of your business growth is difficult because you don't have the financial capacity to hire a lot of staff to handle all the operational aspects of your company. That does not mean you should not examine core elements and streamline them as much as possible to provide room for growth. Even the big primes were once small businesses, and as you grow, you can begin to look and act more like them—as long as you do it with planning and intention.

As a small business owner myself, I get it, and I get it deep in my bones. How much time should I focus on revenue projections, billing, collections, and finances as compared to the actual execution of projects or meeting with clients?

The simple answer is "it depends," and it will vary for each business and change over time. As you experience growth, you will have the capacity to shed some of the tasks that are a burden and you should be delegating. There are legendary management gurus who profess to know just the right words to get you to the promised land. The reality is much different where the rubber hits the road and your time becomes precious and limited.

Let's think about some of the business operations, management ideas, and tools for your toolbox that are routinely used by other successful business owners.

Do, Bill, Collect

It seems like a simple three-step process: Do the work. Bill for the work. Collect your fees for the work performed. We're done here, right? Not so fast. If it was such an easy process, you would never have an issue with cash flow or outstanding receivables or suppliers calling because you are sixty days past due for materials.

Many small business owners started businesses because they got tired of working for someone else, but the internal operations associated with that work were often hidden and mysterious. On top of that, most college and high school programs do not delve into the issue of ensuring you get paid for the work completed. So how does this simple three-step process get put into practice?

To begin, it requires you, as the business owner, or someone on your team, to know what is ongoing and keep detailed records for the individual efforts. That includes payroll, billable expenses, materials, and any other costs that are reimbursable in your contract, which also means a regular review of the contract. From a business operations perspective, I almost universally advise clients to use a payroll service. The weekly or monthly costs are small compared to the headaches of trying to do it yourself. Plus, all that information will be needed by your accountant, insurance broker, and bookkeeper. Build the cost of a payroll service into your overhead costs or billing rates so it does not erode your expected margins; don't be penny wise and pound foolish.

Bill your clients every month. Every month like clockwork. Again, you have to know what your contract calls for with respect to billings. Are you billing on progress and a percentage of completion? Do you have a cost-plus-fixed-fee contract? Are you on a time and materials arrangement? There are a variety of mechanisms and contract types, and having a clear understanding of them will make the billing process that much easier. Regular conversations with your clients will make the process less burdensome; ask them what they need and in what format. In many cases, they can provide a template for your invoices along with the required backup material to substantiate your costs. Don't try to reinvent the wheel or swim upstream. Give clients the information they need in the proper format to eliminate their need to search for the data. You will do yourself a huge service if you establish a schedule for invoicing. Perhaps the goal is to complete the compilation and review of an invoice within ten days of the last Friday of the month, with a goal of submitting it by the fifteenth of the month. There are times to be rigid and times to be flexible. For the financial health of your company and to set expectations, this is the time to be rigid and stick to the schedule. Most clients have a pay cycle and if you miss the date, you have to wait until the following month. Do you want to carry costs for an additional thirty days unnecessarily? Right— neither do I.

The last step is to collect the money for the work you have invoiced. If you are a subcontractor, remember what your agreement stipulates with respect to payments. Typical agreements provide prime contract holders seven to ten days to pay you once they have been paid, which is one more reason you want to get on a regular billing cycle. It is not only important to do the work and bill for it, but you need to have some mechanism to track the bills. If you know it should take about sixty days from the time you submit an invoice to the day you get paid, you need to have some system for knowing when the invoice was actually submitted.

There are a lot of different tools available—MS Excel spreadsheets, QuickBooks, or some other software package—and as long as you pick one that works for you and your business, you will have visibility and transparency. As you see an invoice age a little longer than expected, don't be shy about picking up the phone and asking for an update. Big companies have the same issues as small companies and have the resources to carry the costs, but they don't want to. Calling is just an indication of being aware of your business operations; it reflects a level of professionalism that will be appreciated and admired.

Build The Right Team

You may think the teambuilding activity should be part of human resources, and depending on the part of the team being discussed, you may be right. However, this discussion is about building your external team—not your employees, but the professional service providers that will be integral to the operation of your business.

They will not be picking up a hammer or screwdriver, but their tools and those they help you implement will be as invaluable to building your business as any of the trusted tools in the back of your truck.

When I teach project management workshops, I often offer the following commentary: There is no right answer or solution; there are a range of options with different costs and benefits that have a bearing on the right team. Consider it a moving and changing target. Your needs today are likely not the same as they were three years ago; nor are they the same as they will be in three years' time. There are some constants to consider, though: accountant, attorney, insurance broker, bonding agent. As you grow, you may transition the bookkeeping from a project manager or family member to a dedicated employee, but rest assured, the bookkeeping needs to be done at every stage of maturity of your company.

Your team will include an accountant, a bookkeeper, and a financial planner. This is a perfect time to reinforce some key issues in that regard. It goes without saying that the members of your finance team are invaluable and integral to your personal and professional success. It is critically important to understand the taxman wants his due, and the consequences of not addressing potential tax liabilities can be disastrous. Here are just a few of the potential consequences:

Liens against your company, property, and potentially, your personal assets. Public agencies routinely perform background checks, and liens and judgments will show up. This will restrict their ability to award additional contracts.

 Unpaid taxes are bad, but the penalties and fees are killers. Don't compound a bad situation by racking up, in many cases, costs that are way beyond the original tax bill.

 Unpaid payroll taxes can lead to judgments from the Department of Labor. Don't give a government agency any more reason to ask questions about your business practices than is absolutely necessary.

Get comfortable having regular conversations with your accountant to discuss strategies to minimize your tax bill and exposure. Get in the routine of having at least one check-in call per quarter, preferably after you have provided your quarterly financial statements.

 *When I met Mariana for the first time, she explained she was having trouble getting paid in a timely manner even though she was submitting invoices to her prime on a regular basis. This made her feel restricted about the kind of projects she could pursue. We started pulling the problem apart to figure out what the real issue was. I asked who had reviewed her contract before she signed it and why she felt*

constrained. She admitted, embarrassed, that she just signed the agreement as presented. Her spotty cash flow meant covering payroll and other expenses was a challenge; she felt like she was "robbing Peter to pay Paul" and falling further and further behind. The truth was, she never saw the value in an attorney until it was too late and did not consider a conversation with her accountant about other strategies. Over time, she engaged an attorney to negotiate with her primes and began conversations with her accountant about lines of credit to bridge the lean periods. For Mariana, the situation worked out to her benefit, but she could also have found herself out of business because she did not have the right people advocating and representing her best interests.

Attorneys seem to be an easy target for teasing and ridicule, and for many, their value is not realized until it is too late, or their level of effort is extensive and expensive. In many cases, early intervention and engagement is much less costly than trying to fix a problem once it has been identified. A good attorney will not just fix a problem, but will help you avoid sticky situations in the first place. When you are starting to think about bringing in an attorney to support your company's growth, consider the range of services you will likely need. In a very classic sense, you need a lawyer who understands contracts and negotiations, but you also want one who has a good understanding of your industry. The nuances associated with the public sector, construction, or professional service agreements are varied and hiring just any lawyer is not advised. Find a lawyer who specializes in what you do, understands the lingo, and can foresee some of the risks you may be accepting. You can only imagine the range of topics I discuss with clients, and a good percentage of them relate to legal issues, contracts, or other agreements. I frequently joke with them that I sometimes feel like a half lawyer and there are some family members who would have liked me to go the law school route, especially once dentistry was off the table. Despite the fact that I did not pursue a legal career, I can offer some guidance on potential risks, but recommend my clients speak with professionals who really know what they are talking about when it comes to legal details.

The biggest issue I see by not having an attorney is contracts and agreements that get signed are often one-sided and advantageous to the agency or prime vendor—everything from liquidated damages to payment terms. If you are working directly for an agency, there is less opportunity to get contract terms changed, but the size of the contract may allow for some requirements to be waived. However, the agency may have some latitude to be flexible in circumstances where the risk is considered low or there is no real liability associated with the product or service you are delivering. In cases where you are signing an agreement as a subcontractor, there is frequently more wiggle room in the contract being offered as it relates to surety bonding and payment terms—particularly if your firm is certified and you are helping meet the project's compliance goals. As mentioned before, the standard subcontractor agreement will have "pay when paid" language, but that does not mean the contract holder (if the firm is large enough and inclined to help) can't advance payment to you or allow you to invoice on a biweekly basis to flatten out the cash flow. Bonding is another area worth discussing, and an attorney can be helpful in negotiating better terms or the waiving of requirements. Large primes generally carry large bonds, and for low-value contracts (low value compared to the overall contract and risk), they will often consider covering you under their bonding line. Not always, but sometimes.

In the context of negotiations, it's important to remember if you don't ask, you don't get. (That's a good guideline for marriage, too!) You can't complain about contract terms and the impact on your business if the agreement has not been properly reviewed and adjustments requested. If the agency or prime is unable or unwilling to modify the agreement, you have to ask yourself— in consultation with your team—whether you want to proceed. The sign of maturity in a business owner can be evidenced by the recognition of risks and a willingness to walk away if the potential risk outweighs the ultimate benefits. Just don't try to make all those decisions on your own.

Depending on your actual type of business, insurance and bonding can be a significant component of your monthly expenses and

this extends beyond workers' compensation and general liability. In many cases, you will be expected to carry vehicle insurance or design liability or umbrella policies to fully comply with a contract. First, these costs all need to be considered and accounted for when you develop cost estimates for a potential client. Second, I would encourage you to change the way you view insurance.

Insurance is one of those costs you take on to protect yourself, your employees, your business, and your clients; you hope you never have to exercise it, but it is there to guard against financial ruin. For that reason, try and think about it as a benefit and not a liability. As with any other professional you engage with, find an insurance broker and bonding agent (sometimes one and the same) who is honest and reputable, treats you with respect, and gives you the customer service and time to ensure you are protected. There are bad actors in any industry, so ask around from trusted resources before you agree to work with a particular person. The thing that can almost be guaranteed is that when you start asking around, you will hear a lot of horror stories as well as tales of true professionals who do not cut corners or give short shrift just because you are a smaller company. All the big companies started as small companies, and a good agent will recognize your potential.

Think about this: at one point, Cadillac was considered to have the best customer service in the auto industry. Why? The company understood by treating buyers well, their first purchase would likely lead to lifelong customers valued at nearly $200,000 each in overall sales. Find professionals for your business team who are going to give you Cadillac customer service—those who will be invested in your growth and help you meet your overall goals while protecting you and your assets. Once upon a time, Cadillac was a small auto manufacturer that was able to grow into an icon in the industry. When thinking about icons in the construction industry, rest assured the teams they have developed with internal and external resources have allowed them to grow, reduce their risk, and become more profitable.

What Gets Measured, Gets Managed

Management expert Peter Drucker famously coined that phrase, and for me, this is one of the critical areas associated with business success. I am, after all, a planner and project manager at my core, and really enjoy creating structure and systems. The question "what should I be tracking?" is often thrown to me when I sit on panels for industry events, and my general answer is "as much as you can without creating a hardship." There are any number of activities that should be tracked that will be instructive to your business operations and decision-making process going forward. At a minimum, I advise clients to track the following:

 Work in progress

 Completed projects

 Bids submitted

 Key clients

 *Arjun was a busy contractor with a growing backlog of work who felt like he was burning the candle at both ends, but he couldn't really tell me whether he was meeting his business goals. When we talked about his ongoing projects, he was a little vague about the exact percentages of completion, expected completion dates, and receivables.*

We stopped the conversation right there. I handed him a thumb drive with templates to help him track his projects and rescheduled the meeting for the following week. Over that week, he detailed all the ongoing work, fees received, approved change orders, and projected completion dates. When we sat down the following week, we could see when he would need new projects to begin to keep his staff busy (flattening out the boom-or-bust scenario many contractors experience) and project his cash flow and profitability— and the additional monitoring allowed Arjun to identify potential risks.

There are any number of templates and systems available to track projects and business metrics, and in all honesty, I don't really care which one you choose, as long as you select something. When I worked for a gas utility managing capital construction, I recall a leadership meeting when the president told us he did not care what solution we chose to implement (even if it wasn't his first choice) as long as everyone was on board with it and implemented it consistently. Why? Because even the worst solution implemented with consensus and consistency will yield improvements. So, my general guidance is to select any system and implement it (covering the basics, of course), because any system is better than no system at all.

The tracking template I give to my clients is focused on individual projects, but if you raise the monitoring one level up, you might look at metrics like gross revenue, profit margins, year-over-year growth, distribution of revenue by client, or average project size. These are all examples of key performance indicators (KPIs). The KPIs you select for your company will be uniquely your own, and depending on the type of work you do, can be represented by even simpler numbers. For example, if you are a company that provides professional services, meaning materials are negligible in overall revenue, a substitute for revenue could be the number of employees and their overall billable percentage. I don't know any business owner who can't tell me how many employees are on the payroll—the trickier part will be in modeling the billable percentage target to meet overall revenue and profit margins.

For argument's sake, let's assume there are 2,080 work hours in a year for a full-time employee and each employee gets fifteen days of vacation and sick leave (120 hours) and ten holidays (80 hours). Once those nonbillable or nonproductive hours are removed from the total number of billable hours, each employee without any other responsibilities should be operating at 90 percent productivity. If your employees have billable rates of, for example, $150 per hour, then each employee would generate $282,000 of revenue for a full year. This gives you a general sense of the benefit of adding an additional employee in the professional services environment (construction management, design, and engineering), but the calculation is not as simple in the construction environment because revenue is primarily based on units installed. This is a definite area where creating a flatter workflow will boost profit and productivity without the periods of staff either being overwhelmed or underutilized.

We started with the idea of "what gets measured gets managed" and that still applies, but if you begin developing the metrics for your company, you need to have something to measure it against. That means you need to have some business goals. Some can be simple (adding two new clients this year or hiring a project manager) and some may be detailed (increase profit margins with a key client or deliver all projects on time and on budget), but you will need to know what you are measuring against. Will everything go exactly as planned? Definitely not, and there is rarely straight-line progress. Plan for times when your progress will feel like it's two steps forward and one step back. As a small business owner, it is important to remember to occasionally pick up your head and scan the horizon to make sure you are on the right path. Moving in the right direction, even with some course corrections along the way, will bring the overall success you are trying to achieve.

Align For Now And Plan For Growth

In business school, my classmates and I were reviewing a case study about the nature of businesses and capitalism, and discussed whether there is a case to be made for growing to a certain size and remaining there. Some felt the purpose of a business is to make as much money as possible and grow as large as possible, while others voiced the perspective that staying in a niche was better. Whether you are in the "I'm going to be a captain of industry" camp, the "I like where I am" camp, or someplace in between, it's important to align your business operations with your current situation and plan for growth, whatever that may look like. What am I talking about? Well, we already discussed the need for a team to help manage your business and projects. If you are a $3-million-a-year contractor, you can manage your operations with intermittent help and the likelihood is that you, as the business owner, wear any number of hats—president, COO, CFO, marketing officer, estimator, and project manager. As much as this may seem like a comfortable role, I'm guessing you sometimes feel like a street performer juggling knives, bowling balls, and chainsaws, knowing you have to keep them all in the air to be successful. Quite frankly, it's not really sustainable even if right now it seems to work. What happens if you land that next contract or the larger one after that? Will it still be a manageable situation?

When I work with clients, my goal is to help them be financially effective and to efficiently use the staff and resources available. From a holistic perspective, it is helping the business owner decide between the *need to haves* and the *nice to haves*. I feel like I have seen all types of situations that impact financial performance of a company and some of them leave me scratching my head; I have seen startup companies with minimal revenue operating out of expensive office space under the premise that image is important to potential clients they meet there and wildly successful companies where owners sheepishly invite me to meet in their basement home office. Planning for growth does not mean you need to accommodate for all the growth to occur in the next six to twelve months (i.e., taking on office space and extraneous expenses before they are needed). For me, planning for growth is a function of looking at where you want the company to be and determining what and who will be needed to effectively and efficiently manage it. From a business operations perspective, here are a few areas to plan for:

 Staffing and organization chart—what positions will be needed, roles and responsibilities, cost. More on staffing will be discussed in the chapter on human resources.

 Impact to financial performance—with growth comes increased revenue and increased expenses, though not necessarily in proportion.

 Professional support—accounting, bookkeeping, legal

 Role of the business owner—working *on* the business not *in* the business, strengths and weaknesses

 Union affiliation—a prime consideration for contractors performing public sector projects

Safety First!

Safety goes beyond ensuring your employees arrive at and leave a jobsite the same way—with all their body parts intact. Safety is a mindset best promoted by the business owner that has wide-reaching impacts. Yes, it is important that employees operate safely and are provided the necessary tools to do their job. It also means they are monitored to ensure the tools they are given are actually used. I can recall many, many, many visits to a project site only to find workers without the proper PPE (personal protection equipment) or just choosing not to use it. This includes laborers not wearing safety glasses or reflective vests, inspectors wearing sneakers instead of steel-toed shoes, or a crew leader without a

"I DON'T NEED A HARD HAT, BOSS. I PASSED THE PLUM BOB TEST WHERE THEY DROPPED ONE ON ME FROM 50 STORIES UP AND I SUFFERED NO ILL EFFECTS."

hard hat in sight. Those are not the most harrowing experiences, but likely the most common. In many respects, workers often have a similar attitude as teenagers in that they do not think anything will happen to them if they don't use the PPE because they have been lucky. As a business owner, are you comfortable relying on luck to protect your employees, your assets, or your company?

From a business operations perspective, safety has to be baked into everything you do and everything you talk about, especially with potential clients. So far in this book, we have talked about reporting and information becoming available as it relates to things like liens and judgments, and safety works the same way. OSHA violations are no joke and neither is an EMR rating that will give a prime contractor or agency something to worry about. Your EMR rating (Experience Modification Rate) is used by insurance companies to gauge your past cost of injuries and future chances of risk. Agencies and clients will use your EMR in a similar way. A lack of attention to safety can affect your company in a number of ways.

 It will hinder your ability to differentiate your company from your competitors and secure the contracts you would like to be awarded—and new contracts mean you are moving toward achieving your business goals.

 Your insurance rates will be significantly higher if you have reportable but preventable incidents occurring on your project sites. Higher insurance costs translate into lower profits and money going out the door unnecessarily.

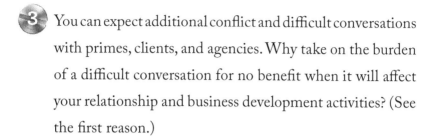 You can expect additional conflict and difficult conversations with primes, clients, and agencies. Why take on the burden of a difficult conversation for no benefit when it will affect your relationship and business development activities? (See the first reason.)

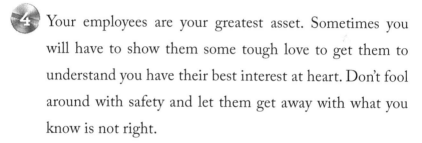 Your employees are your greatest asset. Sometimes you will have to show them some tough love to get them to understand you have their best interest at heart. Don't fool around with safety and let them get away with what you know is not right.

4X4 IN BUSINESS OPERATIONS

As it relates to business operations, 4x4 performance is generally evidenced by a high-performing operation where employees are singing off the same sheet of music and the business owner capably handles the conductor's baton to orchestrate the execution of business activities.

 We can view *competence* through the lens of the business owner and the recognition and acceptance that the job is to work *on* the business. This also means the owner can be self-reflective, acknowledge any deficiencies, and either take the steps to learn more about that area or find someone who can be responsible for it.

 Qualified companies can be seen as meeting or exceeding basic standards. This is reflected in the ability to handle larger projects and the inherent risks (bigger projects translate into increased payrolls and risk associated with carrying those costs), or presenting a track record of safety that gives clients a level of comfort.

 Responsiveness is often seen as taking some form of action or movement in a reactive manner, but as we have discussed, your responsiveness can be seen as your willingness and ability to plan for the future. Planning does not have the same physical component as constructing a building, designing a bridge, or sketching an architectural drawing, but it is just as critical and requires as much brainpower to plan for the future and identify potential pitfalls.

 Be *responsible* in how the work is completed (jobsite safety), in the use of resources (time, money, employees), and the use of professionals to keep your business on track and out of harm's way (lawyers, accountants, insurance agents, business consultants). Are there businesses that succeed without 4x4 performance in this area? I'm sure there are, but movement toward achieving your business goals will accelerate if you can manage your business operations effectively and efficiently. Business operation is often an area that entrepreneurs claim to abhor because it's not creative, exciting, or sexy. Maybe that is the case, but business operations are the cornerstone around which the rest of the organization can be built.

CORNERSTONE QUESTIONS TO SUPPORT YOUR SUCCESS:

- What are the beliefs you hold that are stopping you from asking for what you need to be successful?

- What blind spots do you have in the operational aspects of your business? If you're not sure, who can help you see your blind spots? How are your blind spots protecting you? What are they costing you?

- What would greater proficiency in operations allow you to do with your business?

- What would operational success look like?

CHAPTER 6

Your Communications Tools: Relationship Building, One Conversation At A Time

Everybody has their own personal communication styles, for better *and* for worse. For some, it means yelling across a construction site with only a slightly lower volume once they get back into the office. For others, it amounts to text messages and short emails when a brief phone call or face-to-face conversation would be much more effective. Some address conflict immediately and directly, while others hold off on dealing with difficult situations in the hopes that they will resolve themselves.

While construction is often viewed through the lens of making progress, completing physical tasks, and applying a specific set of skills and abilities to make a project come to life, the ability to communicate effectively can often be the differentiator between success and failure. If we begin to think about where communications, good and bad, come into play in the management and growth of a business, there are few areas where it is critical to meet business goals. Whether it is in your interactions with customers or clients, providing direction and feedback to staff, or making requests of vendors or subcontractors, the how, when, and why are important to consider.

Throughout this chapter, you will find situations and examples of where communication is an integral part of managing relationships for growth, clarity, and transparency. Consider your own interactions with clients and prime contractors. What tools have they picked up along the way and put to use to influence others, supervise project teams, or get their message across that have enabled them to expand their business? If you want to build like the big primes, sometimes you have to communicate like them for your message to be heard.

The Customer Is Always Right

It seems as though this is the message we have all come to accept—the customer is always right, and as a contractor, there is no opportunity to disagree or question decisions that affect the work being completed. Now, I am not suggesting it is a good idea to challenge everything, and I would caution that it takes tact and forethought before jumping into a difficult conversation with an agency, client, or prime contractor. There is a natural hierarchy, but assuming you have made enough goodwill deposits in the relationship bank account with the client, there will likely be enough trust built up that will allow for a dissenting opinion. Even so, the manner in which the conversation unfolds is important to consider, as well as the language selected to convey your thoughts.

My client Rachel had been working on a project as a prime contractor for the first time with a particular agency. As the work progressed, the agency made material changes to the project and design conflicts were identified that prevented the project from being built as it was shown on the plans. The result? The project was taking longer than scheduled and the changes were having a financial effect on the awarded contract amount. What was she to do? How could she make all of this known? We strategized for a while to make sure the conversation did not devolve into finger-pointing, or as I have heard throughout my career, "throwing someone

under the bus." By the time we were done talking about the situation, Rachel had some reasonably good approaches to bringing the issues to the client's attention, along with some ways to get the project back on track.

The approach to the conversation had little to do with assigning blame, but was aimed at creating a collaborative atmosphere where she could express her concerns, identify what she saw as some of the challenges, and discuss the various options available. Could they fix everything? No, but they could make some things better. The client appreciated the honesty and transparency of the conversation and the sense that the contractor was there to do its job, was not trying to generate additional work, and did not view the client as a cash register with the drawer open and nobody there to make sure there was no theft. The client also appreciated that the issues were not raised for the first time at a large monthly progress meeting, where others might be put on the spot unnecessarily. The issues were initially raised in a small group setting with the relevant players, and once the topics were raised, the client approved adding it to the agenda of the upcoming meeting.

Here are some things to remember when communicating with a client or customer:

Communicate early and often. As soon as a problem arises, or even as a problem can be seen on the horizon, bring your client into the conversation. It may start with the phrase, "There is not a problem now, but . . ." or, "We have been reviewing our progress against the schedule . . ." The presentation demonstrates planning, forethought, and respect for the client and the project.

There will be bad news; accept it as a reality. Bad news can be a two-way street. Sometimes the client needs to delay a project that may affect other parts of the business or tell you about an employee who has done something wrong on the jobsite. As a contractor, the bad news may be about a delay in material deliveries or a subcontractor becoming unavailable. Understand nobody likes getting bad news—or delivering bad news for that matter—but through developing a solid professional relationship based on honesty and common goals, the sting can be reduced.

"WHAT DO YOU MEAN WE CAN'T FINISH ON TIME?
DO YOU WANT HISTORY TO SAY THAT
ROME WASN'T BUILT IN A DAY?"

Feedback is critical to continued growth and success. All too often, when the project ends, everyone is so tired, happy, and ready to move on that there is little interest in sitting down and going through the lessons learned. In the industry, we are great about talking about lessons learned and less great about actually applying them. In the same way an employee should be evaluated for performance and then given goals for improvement, a valued client should be willing to do the same, and most likely, will be open to giving feedback throughout the project when there is still an opportunity to address their concerns. And remember, it's not personal; it's just business and you want to be in the business of accepting feedback gracefully—even when you disagree.

Without your employees, you can't function. Many of the same concepts related to communications with a client can be applied to the manner in which employees are addressed. The interesting part of a business is the value is often tied to physical assets, while the less tangible assets are left to flourish or wither on their own. In the construction industry, a company may be valued by cash on hand, receivables, work in place but not yet invoiced, equipment and tools, signed contracts, and leases. Rarely does a bank or bonding agent delve too deeply into your staff—their longevity, skill sets, or overall engagement. Employee communications, more specifically, *effective* employee communications, can go a long way toward keeping and growing your staff, helping them become more effective and proficient, and reducing the cost of continually searching for new staff to replace departed staff. As the adage goes, it is cheaper to keep a client happy then to acquire a new client; the same is true when it comes to staff.

Bob's concrete business was growing, and in the span of a year, he had won three new contracts, which meant more jobsites, more administration, more clients to talk to, and less time to spend with the crews in the field. He had always made a point of visiting the active sites at least a couple of times a week and could be counted on for a good joke, fresh donuts, and an update on what was happening with the company. His crews recall him pulling on work boots to help out in a pinch and they respected that. When we met, he told me one of his guys recently left to go to another company. Did he leave for money? No. Better benefits? No. He left because, with all the growth, he felt disconnected and that he was no longer worth Bob's time. Bob had missed out on an important opportunity with his crews to "bring them along" and articulate the big picture. He showed up to each site the next week to let them all know how integral they were to the overall success of the business and how he planned to keep them in the loop—and they enjoyed their donuts, too.

What is communicated to employees, in what manner, and at what time, is key to effective employee communications. Employees are not entitled to know everything about the company they work for, but as it affects them, they have to be kept apprised. That communication can be about a new project coming up that will require overtime or night work, a significant change from the current work schedule, or any other topic that will affect employees—such as changes in the industry that will affect all employees but the company can't control, like new OSHA and site safety guidelines. As for Bob, he needed to communicate what was happening with growth and what changes were expected (e.g., new PMs, policies or procedures).

Bankers, Accountants, And Lawyers, Oh My!

There are some who strictly view lawyers, accountants, bankers, bonding agents, and the like as necessary evils or a means to an end. However, building out your team to include these professionals will help protect the business and facilitate its growth. But we are talking about communications in this chapter and in a word— honesty. These are supporting members of the business team, and if they are kept in the dark, lied to, or ignored, their overall ability to help you meet your business goals will drop significantly. There are often questions about frequency, content, and the manner in which you communicate with these professionals and the answer is generally "it depends," though there are some ideas to consider and tailor for your business and situation.

Priya was on top of her business and finances and could easily describe her workflow and backlog for the coming six months. All good until I pushed her a little harder on what her accountant was planning for the expected profits by year end. Priya told me she had her bookkeeper send the monthly financials to the accountant and she had not heard anything, so she assumed everything was fine. She might have been right, but her assumption did not take into account that silence is not always golden; it was possible tax issues could be looming. Her communication with a critical service provider had been left to an employee, and there had been no follow-up by Priya to check in. We talked about implementing a more proactive approach to managing the accountant and her other service providers, as well as breaking down the silos to allow them to communicate with each other.

There is a tendency to only communicate with these types of professionals when there is a problem (think project liens or letters from the IRS or Department of Labor, for example) or when there is a pressing need (a project award that requires bonding significantly higher than current limits). As a result, you create a crisis situation that requires them to drop everything—if they will even do that for you. If you have selected the right people to support you and your company, they are more than willing to schedule a brief call to keep you apprised of what's going on and the outlook for the future. Brief means brief—fifteen to thirty minutes should do the trick—and I recommend an actual call even when there is no pressing need. (We will talk about email and text versus phone and in-person later.) In general, a quarterly call may be enough for them to have a sense of what support you will need, and ensure you they will be available when you need them. Here are some ideas to consider implementing:

Share without oversharing. In the age of Facebook, most of us can point to friends or acquaintances who cannot make that distinction and as a result you are aware of all the minutia of their lives—things you don't care about or have any reason to know. With these professionals, their time is valuable (just as your own is) and there is no reason to share more than they need to know. If one happens to be a personal friend, save the longer and personal conversations for weekends or evenings.

Trust, but verify. President Ronald Reagan famously coined the phrase as it related to the former Soviet Union and the agreements it was entering into with the United States. In the context of trust and verification, have your regularly scheduled call, but follow up with an email to confirm the details and next steps. You hire specialists because they have expertise in a particular area. It will often happen that you will believe you understand a situation until the phone call ends. If you can restate the topics discussed and have the other person concur, you are on your way to a much clearer line of communication.

Better safe than sorry. Ask your professional service providers what their preferred method of communication is and make sure you can find some common ground. As a busy business owner, the tendency is often to communicate through text messages and exceedingly brief emails as a thought comes into your head. Most service providers are likely going to want and need more detail, forethought, and time than you may have while standing on a loud construction site. This is a completely reasonable thing to ask even before the relationship begins as you interview them—like you would a potential employee.

Avoid The Game Of Telephone

I have fond and not-so-fond memories of elementary school when at the beginning of each school year the teacher would engage the class with ice breakers, and inevitably, a game of telephone with twenty-five students. The first student whispers a word or phrase to the second in line and so forth until the message reached the last in line. Without fail, whatever the last person reported bore little resemblance to the first person's statement. It happens for many reasons in all sorts of adult situations, too, including a company, office, or construction site. Why is it that we don't all hear the same thing? There could be language barriers or strong accents; there could be an inherent bias; it could be overconfidence or an unwillingness to ask for clarification or repetition; or it could just be that a verbal message does not register in the same way a written message does.

Carol's firm was part of the winning bid for a large building overhaul and her specialty, painting, naturally came at the end of the overall project. Over the course of months, she would regularly call the prime contractor and ask about when her work would get plugged in and whether there were any changes to the schedule. Her client kept reassuring her everything was on track and he was meeting with the agency regularly. He neglected to tell Carol about scope changes that affected the work her crews would be completing. When the work finally came her way, the schedule was shortened to meet the overall completion date, something that required unexpected overtime and resulted in an unhappy agency when it learned of the projected cost overrun. Looking back, the situation could have been clarified if the monthly reports sent to the agency had also been sent to all subcontractors for transparency and inclusion.

There are communications to put in writing and others to be discussed in person or over the phone. In Carol's case, she was asking the right questions and was, in her mind, getting straight answers. If you are working for a public agency or large entity (either as a subcontractor or prime contractor), there will generally be monthly reports or schedule updates provided to clients to let them know of any potential problems. Don't be shy about asking for a copy to protect your own interests. In the previous section, I addressed how and when to communicate with your lawyer, and while I am *not* a lawyer, many advise documenting issues as they arise during a project. That is a universally accepted approach for good project management and self-protection, but it does not require you to transmit that information—consider it your internal communications if things happen to go badly. Here are a few tips to consider or remember when it comes to written and verbal communications:

Email has no context or emotion. Unless you happen to be in the habit of typing in all caps or using emojis like punctuation, it is hard for the reader to know your state or mind, tone of voice, or intended nuance. (Note: Emojis have no real place in business communications except for the occasional smiley face to accompany "Happy Monday" or "Have a great weekend"—and that's with someone you know fairly well.) The same is true for text messages, so be careful when using these forms of written communications if you have concerns about your message being misinterpreted or muddled. It is the manner in which the reader interprets the message that is really the most important factor, so write for clarity. We are living in an ever more digital world and one only needs to pick up a newspaper to read about the discovery of incriminating information in email and text messages. What you type and how it is interpreted could be used as evidence should something go wrong. It is always good to read and re-read a message before pressing send.

When in doubt, pick up the phone. I'm a big fan of using the actual telephone—I know, how 1990s of me—especially if the topic to be discussed has some sensitivity associated with it. It can be a little tricky to determine when a situation is sensitive and should first be discussed in private before committing it to paper or email. What sort of issues should or could fall into this category? Consider employee performance or other personnel matters, budget and schedule conflicts, potential problems, and the like. It will convey a sense of seriousness and bring the other person into the situation as your partner in identifying solutions.

Don't editorialize. You may get to the point when you have to document a difficult situation for your prime, client, or employee. As Joe Friday would say as a detective in *Dragnet*, "Just the facts, ma'am." Go with the facts, whether it is a monthly progress report, employee evaluation, or after-action report due to a safety violation or accident. There are plenty of opportunities to have that discreet conversation you don't want to have in public.

Know Your Audience

There is an old adage that says, "There are two types of speakers: those who are nervous and those who are liars." In other words, everyone gets nervous at some point when asked to make a presentation. Inevitably, you will be asked to speak in public, present at a large meeting, pitch your company to a new client, or attend a pre-bid meeting where you have to introduce yourself and your company. And yes, we all get nervous; even the best public speakers have some level of anxiety when they are in that setting. The difference between an average person and a more seasoned speaker is the level of preparation, time spent practicing, and knowing what to expect. In preparation, it is always helpful to ask yourself the following questions: Who will be there? What message do I want to get across? How much time will I be speaking? What outcome am I hoping for?

Abdul was nervous when I spoke to him in the days leading to a conference; the first thing out of his mouth was "why did I agree to sit on this panel?" He had never sat on a panel before and was concerned about how he would be perceived by the audience. He had seen other panelists in action at other conferences and knew how they came off—cool, calm, and collected. Having been in his situation myself and having served as a panel moderator, I gave him some advice from my own experience. I recommended we spend some time with practice questions to get him more comfortable, even though we did not know the actual questions. This gave him greater self-confidence—in his technical expertise and his ability to deliver crisp, concise answers to the conference attendees.

In some cases, the audience is known, and many times you will know some or all of the attendees at a meeting, so you can take some comfort in seeing a few friendly faces. It is important to present with confidence and deliver a clear, consistent message with the end goal in mind. In construction, we often throw around the term "means and methods" freely, though it generally refers to the manner in which a project will be built. This same concept can be adapted to public speaking and delivering a sharp and targeted message. The "means" can be viewed in the context of the setting (i.e., conference, meeting, pitch, networking event) and the "methods" would be the manner in which the information is conveyed (i.e., formal stand-up presentation with PowerPoint, formal meeting in a conference room, casual setting in a client's office, or an industry networking event where you are unscripted). Consider these points:

Do your research. When thinking about delivering your message and working through your means and methods, do your research on who may be at the meeting and what will be most important to them. You may be asked to present your project at a conference or industry event where attendees may be most interested in what made it successful and the lessons learned. In a meeting with potential clients, you might want to focus on how you can help relieve their potential "pain points." Ask yourself, "what is keeping this audience up at night?" and make sure your presentation addresses that.

What is your POV? Your POV is your personal point of view, your perspective, how you see things. For the most part, your audience wants to know what makes you different, unique, and perhaps even special. Your POV is a result of your personal and professional experiences, your ways of approaching a situation, and your personality. Don't be afraid to share your POV and let others know you do not subscribe to a cookie-cutter mentality.

Picture yourself as a newspaper reporter. As you think about your audience, consider the five Ws + one H of reporting—who, what, where, when, why, and how.

Who will you be speaking to, so you can adjust your message accordingly?

 What information do you want them to have, and what impression do you want to impart?

 Where will you be addressing the audience—conference room, auditorium, trade show, networking event, etc.?

 When will you be making your pitch? As much as possible, be aware of the time of day, day of the week, and other factors that could dilute your message's impact. Late in the day on a Friday or right before lunch might not be ideal for maximum attention.

 Why are you being invited to speak to this audience and what might be expected of you?

 How do you intend to address the audience and what materials will enhance your message. Materials can include a company brochure, capability statement, printed presentation, or photos of success stories. (Even failures can be used as a success if you can show learning and growth.)

Practice, practice, and practice some more. Most professionals put significantly more time and energy into getting the materials perfect (an attractive PowerPoint, an eye-catching handout, etc.) and significantly less time practicing having the actual words come out of their mouths before the big day. That's a mistake. You don't want the first time that you're attempting to convert your thoughts into spoken words to be in front of others. Do a few rounds of practice aloud before you present to an audience. It will be noticeable if you do this—and even more noticeable if you don't.

Can We Measure Effective Communications?

We start getting into interesting territory when we think about how or if we can measure effective communication. At first thought, most would say you can't really measure effective communication— there are no numbers or indicators that can be examined. I would argue there is ample data you can look at to determine whether you are presenting (communicating) your case in a thoughtful, cogent, and clear manner.

As the owner of a growing business, I encourage you to track your projects from a financial perspective, and on the project execution side of the equation, I would guess most clients require the maintenance of logs (requests for information, change orders, requests for clarification, etc.) for clarity and transparency. This is an example of highly formalized communications and can be measured with respect to identifying an issue, raising it with a client, and getting resolution. For example, let clients know at the start of projects that making alterations after the actual construction has started and the work is in place that it will cost, on average, 150x *more* than the cost if changes are identified before building starts. Effectively communicating in this way with your clients provides you with the opportunity to save them money and be the hero on the project team.

You can also view effective communications with your employees through a review of their performance and their ability to understand your directions. If you find they are not always doing as you wish, perhaps a review of your own communication style and method of communications could be instructive in understanding the crossed wires. Communication tools might be thought of as sophisticated or discretionary, but our near-constant communications up, down, and across organizations makes them important tools to master and use every day.

4X4 IN COMMUNICATIONS

What does it mean to be a 4x4 performer when it comes to communications?

 Competent communication means you have taken care of the basics when it comes to delivering a clear, concise, and consistent message to your customers, clients, agencies, vendors, and employees. It also includes the process of determining who you are speaking to, the message you want to deliver, and linking it to the message they want and need to hear.

 Qualified includes the incorporation of the five Ws and one H in any message you are putting out—in a presentation, phone call, proposal, or email, or at a networking event. As you put the concepts into practice, they will become part of who you are and you won't even notice yourself going through a mental checklist.

 Responsive contractors, when it comes to communications, are proactive rather than reactive. You want to anticipate your clients' needs and try and get ahead of them. But being responsive to a call, email, or business opportunity does not mean reacting so quickly that you have not had time to consider the situation; sometimes, it just means acknowledging the request and setting an expectation for a response. Responsive also means being willing and able to adapt your style to others' preferences.

 Responsible contractors say what they mean and mean what they say. They set expectations and will have difficult conversations, when necessary. But being responsible—and practicing or getting help—means you can find a way to take the sting out of a tough conversation. They also hold themselves responsible for the impact they have on others (whether intended or unintended), and take steps to correct misunderstandings and repair relationships sooner rather than later.

CORNERSTONE QUESTIONS TO SUPPORT YOUR SUCCESS:

- Where do you consistently get positive feedback about your communication style? Where do you get negative feedback—or no feedback at all?

- How do you know when your messages are well-received and on-target? How do you know when they're not?

- Who are the most effective communicators you know, and what can you learn from them?

- What small changes can you experiment with to communicate more effectively with employees, clients, vendors, or service providers?

CHAPTER 7

Your Personal Branding Tools: Put Your Best Foot Forward

When we think about branding, it's easy to get lost in the search for the perfect logo, website design, or business card layout. But when we go down that rabbit hole, we lose sight of what branding is really all about.

Yes, there is a part of branding that is about the websites and logos, but at its core, branding is really about how you present yourself and your company to the outside world. So, it is important to think about personal branding as well as company branding.

Personal branding is about your self-confidence, self-esteem, and self-image. These may not seem relevant to the growth of the company, the completion of projects, or the pursuit of new opportunities. However, as a small business owner, your personal brand and the company brand are intertwined in a way you may not find with the big primes. For bigger firms, the company brand overtakes the personal brand with growth and expansion, even though at a local office there may be a big personality associated with the company. For you, while your company is growing, there is a benefit to mingling personal and company brands because *you* are the person people trust—or don't.

Chief Cook And Bottle Washer

Even if your business card says "president," "CEO," or some other executive position, your title may not match your physical appearance, attitude, or image. And that diminishes your personal and professional credibility. As a small business owner—we already talked about the change in language from "contractor" to "business owner"—there are dozens of responsibilities and items on your to-do list that never seem to get completed, but that does not mean the outside world needs to know that you're under constant stress.

Think about a duck floating along in a pond. Above the water, the duck appears calm and peaceful, but under the water it is paddling like crazy to get from one side to the other. From a personal branding perspective, you want to appear as a duck, quietly floating on the pond without letting people see the frantic splashing below the water line as you try to stay afloat.

Al is a great carpenter—more than just a carpenter, really, who has been steadily growing his company since he went out on his own five years ago. He routinely pursues and wins interior renovation contracts and has a clear sense of the right work for him and his company. His brand—what he is known for—is all about quality and delivering projects as promised. He is a trusted partner to his clients and gets a lot of projects through word of mouth, recommendations, and solid relationships. Al had the company brand locked down tight. However, Al always seemed to be scrambling to get invoices to the client in a timely manner, his car (mobile office) was scattered with random receipts, and he always appeared at his wits' end. Al would typically arrive just as meetings were set to begin and looked as if he had just stepped off a construction site wearing dirty boots, pants, and often-stained t-shirts—not necessarily the image of a business owner. When I asked my colleague Anita about her

experience with Al, she had nothing but praise for him as a contractor—but did not perceive him as a business owner or executive.

Even if you're working in construction, appearance counts. Whether in a large organization, small company, or startup, the adage "dress for the job you want, not the job you have" never seems to go out of style. These adages endure, unlike bell bottoms and platform shoes, because they have withstood the test of time and provide a good reminder about self-image, attitude, and approach. While Al was making money (real profit, not just revenue), he had not considered how he was viewed by his clients, and that the view went beyond skin deep. He was not seen as a CEO or president because he was still trying to do everything himself, which meant some things slipped through the cracks. The risk Al ran was that the perception might become reality and the perception of his ability—and by extension that of his business—was that he was not ready to take on bigger opportunities; his clients were experiencing a crisis of confidence. It was part organizational and part appearance and attitude. Getting some help to meet some basic needs that he personally did not have to handle freed him up to be more strategic. After all, the leader of an organization has to set the vision and be strategic. Acting the part is the first step in creating the image of being a leader or executive, and eventually perception becomes reality.

Consider these points:

Dress for success. You may not want to wear your Sunday best when the schedule for the day involves meeting with crews on a project site. But that also does not mean you should dress as if you will be digging a hole or placing concrete. A good guideline for attire is: neat and clean. That might mean jeans and a golf shirt or blouse. If you are scheduled to meet a client after visiting a job site it is easy enough to have a change of shoes and blazer to throw over a clean shirt for a greater sense of professionalism. If you are meeting with clients, as you might if you were going for job interviews, do a little research to understand their culture and reflect it accordingly. Zappos, the Las Vegas-based online footwear and apparel company, has a no-tie policy, and if you show up wearing one, they will famously take scissors to it and tack it up on the wall. They take their business seriously, but also place a premium on fun and personal expression—and ties definitely do not fit their attitude. And if you show up wearing one, it also means you haven't done your research! The bottom line is that you can present yourself in a positive way by dressing for the occasion—which is part of knowing your audience.

Never let them see you sweat. This tagline for a deodorant goes back to the idea of being the duck paddling furiously below the water while having a calm appearance above. It may be hard work to portray yourself as cool, calm, and collected, and it's worth it.

Your clients do not need to know what happens behind the scenes of your company—and you don't want to give them a reason to ask. It is best to present a get-it-done attitude and then figure out how to actually get it done. Of course, don't be afraid to ask for help in getting it done. Asking for help is a sign of strength, not weakness.

Be Ready Now (Even if You Aren't Really Ready) You may have to play the part of the business executive until you have the resources, skills, or mindset to *be* the business executive. It can be a difficult transition to make from tactical and operational thinking to strategic thinking, especially when people are depending on you. When the time is right, show off those CEO skills by asking the right questions at the right time so you can be seen the way you want to be seen—as a partner, problem solver, trusted advisor, and leader.

Employees Are A Reflection Of Their Leaders

What message are your staff members sending every day when they arrive at the office or jobsite? Do they arrive on time and ready to work? Tom Coughlin, the legendary NFL coach for the New York Giants and Jacksonville Jaguars, pushed the approach that the players arrive at 9:50 a.m. for a 10 a.m. meeting. For him, "on time" was ten minutes early. If staff is arriving just at the start time, they are not actually prepared to start work at the appointed time. Are they organized and neat in their work and in the manner in which they are dressed? Would you be proud if your client dropped in on the jobsite to observe your employees or talk to them about the task at hand? If these questions are making you a little nervous, perhaps your employees do not accurately reflect your company's values and image and there is opportunity to make improvements.

Jimena has real attention to detail in managing her business, interacting and responding to clients, and finding new projects. After many calls with her, I am now accustomed to my phone ringing sixty to ninety seconds before our appointed time. She once told me that when time is precious, those first two minutes give her the chance to get the pleasantries out of the way and get down to business. This approach impressed me, and on a scheduled meeting at one of her jobsites, she got very quiet when she saw how her employees arrived. The superintendent was there early, but her workers showed up at 7:30 a.m. for the start of the day—they are scheduled for a 7:30 a.m. to 3:30 p.m. shift— and the way they looked did not represent her company in the way she wanted. She turned and asked sheepishly, "They are construction workers, right?" despite knowing that their untied sneakers and ripped pants gave a terrible impression. We talked about a range of strategies, and over the course of a few weeks, she got them looking better with company T-shirts and more frequent toolbox talks on the importance of appearance and professionalism—even for construction workers.

A lax or disorganized attitude from the owner will invariably lead to a comparable attitude among the troops, likely not one a business owner would be proud to display. In a "dirty business"— and I am thinking of Mike Rowe from *Dirty Jobs* and not those involved in illegal or immoral activities— the ability to maintain an orderly appearance helps in the branding of the company because many more people will see your employees than will see you on a regular basis. In the same way your goal is to deliver your projects on time, on budget, and to the satisfaction of your clients, you want your employees to hold those goals for themselves by showing up to work on time, prepared, and proud of their ability to get the job done—even if they will leave the site covered in dirt, mud, or sawdust.

Consider these points:

Be consistent. The cost of branded T-shirts for your employees to wear on jobsites is pretty low compared to your company losing business because your employees are seen as unprofessional. The benefits of the T-shirts are free advertising, standardization of attire, and projecting a consistent and positive image. Beyond the cosmetic, ensuring your staff has the proper and appropriate safety equipment is paramount to exuding an air of quality and attention to detail. Some companies will pay for boots for their employees; yes, they can be pricey, but it is something to consider if you can work it into the budget. Don't forget to arm your foreperson or superintendent with extra hard hats, gloves, safety glasses, and reflective vests. A well-equipped worker will stand out from the crowd.

Lead by example. When you visit your jobsites, you should follow the same rules your employees are expected to follow. Show up early for a status meeting so you can catch up with your workers and learn about and see any potential hot-button issues. If they need safety gear to be on the site, you do as well. Speak to them respectfully and professionally. Just because they are involved in manual labor does not mean they are not entitled to the respect and deference you would give a bookkeeper, project manager, or assistant. In an industry that is becoming ever more diverse it is even more important to ensure your own language is clean and that you are not using terms that may once have been considered acceptable, but are now considered offensive. This can include cursing (not all are comfortable with blue language, racist labels, sexist references, or homophobic remarks). This is not about being politically correct, but about being inclusive and sensitive to others around you.

Empower your employees. Most business owners want their employees to take initiative, solve problems, and represent the company appropriately. Often, this comes down to communication and language. How do you want your staff to communicate to a vendor or client? How should they respond to a request to do out-of-scope work? The manner in which they reply will say more about the company, and you as a leader, than the content of the answer. Give them guidance and set some clear expectations—and positive reinforcement won't hurt, either. Construction can be a rough industry and the language you hear on a jobsite might make a sailor blush—so making your employees conscious of this will help portray the company in a more professional light.

Show, don't tell. I can only imagine the amount of time and energy that is invested in finding just the right color or logo to represent what a company is all about. I am a huge fan of the TV show *American Pickers*, where lifelong friends Mike and Frank travel the United States in a van, searching barns and garages for rusty treasures to buy for resale in their stores. On one episode, the guys were "picking" an optometrist's garage and they found a gold mine of advertising material related to eyeglasses. Outside his shop, the owner had an enormous pair of eyeglasses that lit up to let passersby know what he sold. He explained in the period of immigration at the turn of the twentieth century, it was common to use icons or images to attract customers—not for the beauty or quality of the image, but because many new arrivals to America could not read English. When people saw a barber's pole, a boot, or a needle and thread, they would instantly know what service the shopkeeper provided. Does that mean your logo should be entirely tied to your profession? Not necessarily, but it certainly can. The greater level of specialization, the more appropriate it would be.

Nancy is a painting contractor. She is not a general contractor, she does not provide carpentry services, and she is happy in her niche as a subcontractor on larger projects or pursuing projects related to painting. As part of the assessment of her business and development of a business plan, we talked about her branding. As you might imagine, painters are generally about one thing—color. When we sat to review her materials (business cards, giveaways, capability statement, logo, and letterhead), I was struck by the muted tones and lack of an icon to tie back to her line of business. Without going to an extreme that did not fit her personality, we found an image (a paintbrush) to tell potential clients what she does and added a more vibrant color palette to attract the eye.

Of course, clients are not hiring you because of your slick logo or creative color scheme. They hire you because of your experience, expertise, and quality. However, companies do need to stand out from the crowd, and your logo and colors may be the first impression potential clients get about you and your company. Being professional matters, because you don't get a second chance to make a good first impression. I am not a graphic designer and would have a hard time differentiating between various color shades, but I can recognize a clean, clear, and relevant logo and color scheme. As I have often advised my teenage son Jacob, neon orange socks and red sneakers generally do not make a good combination (and he, naturally, ignores me, and figures out how to make it work for his own personal style).

Let your fingers do the walking. The tagline originally referred to the Yellow Pages, which are rarer to find in the internet age. However, let your fingers do the work of finding online resources for logos and color schemes that will be appropriate.

When we think about the purpose of a business card, it is quite literally to provide someone with a way to contact you, so it includes your basic business information—it shouldn't be a flyer. Turning the card into a NASCAR vehicle with a dizzying array of images and colors is not going to work to your advantage. Think about how it will be perceived by the person you meet at a networking event.

One place I have found helpful that does not require hiring a graphic designer is Vistaprint. When it comes to creating business cards, the site has a wealth of stock logos and associated palettes to choose from—and you can download the logo for multiple uses. And of course, there are many other options as well. Find the one that works best for your style, timing, and budget.

Less is more sometimes. If two colors are good, then four will be better, right? Personally, I would prefer a sharp logo with fewer colors to reduce the distraction a more expansive array of colors can cause. Of course, if your brand is all about color, like my painting contractor, by all means use more colors, but use them judiciously to tell the story of what you do.

4X4 IN BRANDING

Are you on your way to being a 4x4 performer in your branding efforts?

 Competent contractors use branding to tell a story about the company and accentuate good work being done for clients. Whether it is the personal branding of the owner in terms of appearance, demeanor, and attitude, or the professionalism displayed by the field staff, good branding happens all day, every day and is the result of conscious choices.

 Qualified contractors recognize the value of presenting a positive image and go beyond the basics of selecting any logo or color palette. They understand the need to integrate branding into all elements of the business, from client communications to managing employees, and projecting an image of being a business owner instead of just a contractor.

 Responsive contractors have an eye out for potential conflicts between perception and reality. Eventually, the two converge, so if the perception is bad, that will set in as the reality for your clients, employees, and vendors. As a business owner, being responsive involves addressing problems early to prevent negative effects on the company brand.

 Responsible owners and executives are open to feedback and are willing to make changes. The creation and nurturing of a positive brand can be lost in the blink of an eye if care is not taken to protect it and ensure a consistent message from top to bottom on the organizational chart.

CORNERSTONE QUESTIONS TO SUPPORT YOUR SUCCESS:

- What are you doing to create the best image of yourself and your company? What can you do differently to have others see you how you want to be seen?

- Who has the best branding in your industry and what can you learn from that?

- How might a change in personal or company branding offer you greater opportunities?

- Who outside your company can give you feedback on your current branding?

- What words or language are you using that you should stop using? What impact may those words be having on your image, your employees or your clients?

CHAPTER 8

Your Marketing Tools: Put Yourself Into The Marketplace

I often get calls from companies looking for help with their marketing efforts. This is sometimes a request to make introductions to larger companies or agencies with which they know I have a relationship. At other times, it's to help them complete a proposal or bid for a project they are pursuing. I sometimes think the use of the word "marketing" does not actually fully encompass the range of activities—physical and deep thought—that need to be considered.

Marketing is so much more than promoting your company, having the perfect website, and a thick stack of business cards you have collected that you thumb through periodically as a reminder of people you meant to follow up with. When I think about marketing as it pertains to a small construction company, I start with purpose and core competencies. I already talked about business owners who could not articulate *why* or *how* they got into business, but it is equally important to have a clear vision of the *what* your business is all about. Right about now, you may be scratching your head and going, "Huh? I thought this was about marketing," and trust me, it *is* about marketing. We are going to dig into your *what*, the purpose of your business, and then talk about how you find the *what* you are seeking—profitability, of course.

Larger companies have the ability to go after a lot of potential projects; their staff have the bandwidth to crank out bids because they have the infrastructure in place and the network of subcontractors to call for estimates. Your key marketing tool, the one you keep in your back pocket at all times, is the one that gets you into a select network of subcontractors so the phone calls come to *you*. You may want to become the big prime on the block putting together the overall bid, in which case you need to learn a lot about the rules, regulations, and bid requirements, or you may be perfectly happy in your niche as a preferred vendor. Either way, your marketing tools can always be refreshed to consider changes in the industry, upcoming opportunities, new technologies, and the power of a personal phone call.

What Do You Do?

So, let's talk about your *what.* What do you do? What are you best at? What makes your company ideally positioned to deliver the kind of projects you are pursuing? You can think of this as your elevator pitch, though, to be honest, I don't really believe in trying to distill what you do and your value proposition down to a tightly rehearsed thirty-second version that eliminates all your personality, charm, and emotion. However, you have to refine the purpose of your company to a point where you know what you can and should be pursuing—and you can talk about it with confidence and ease.

Richard owns a small construction company and has grown over the years to the point that, when I met him and asked what he does, he responded, "I'm a GC." With a little poking, he admitted he had recently begun the transition from residential and commercial projects to pursuing projects with municipalities and public agencies. He could see the concern on my face and wanted to know why. I suggested to him that he might have the capacity to take on the role of a general contractor with smaller projects, but not the financial capacity, risk tolerance, or infrastructure to take on that role with a large, public project. My next questions brought a smile to his face. "What is the work you would take any day of the week with the confidence that you can complete it on time, on budget, and to the satisfaction

of your client?" It turns out his core business was interior construction, and he had a great project manager who had been with him for a long time. That was his what.

There is tremendous value in being aspirational, looking to the future, and planning for growth, *and* you want to ensure you build the plan on a solid foundation of knowledge and acknowledgment of what you do well. A case can be made to just focus on your *what*, but we will talk about that later. As you examine your assets, including your personal experience and expertise, your staff abilities, your client base, and your successful and not-so-successful projects, you will probably start to see some recurring themes. For example:

 We did well when we completed the concrete formwork and placement on this project because we had an excellent safety inspector.

 Our estimating work for this client saved them time and money on the project through alternative construction methods.

 The schedule was shortened for the delivery of electrical equipment through coordination and communication with our vendors and manufacturers.

Project planning and pre-construction services resulted in a project the owner and the community could both support.

Too often, I meet with business owners who are akin to the kid who sees the giant ice cream sundae, and whose eyes are bigger than his stomach. Having a bigger vision of what is possible should be encouraged as long as you can deliver on a 4x4 perspective with the services you offer and provide. Your *what* has to be done with quality and competence. Over time, you can definitely expand the range of services and plan for the increased scope; it is a critical component to being ready when the opportunity arises. For the near term, it will serve you well to refine the picture of what you do well and where you can deliver value to your clients.

What exactly does the *what* have to do with marketing? Excellent question and I'm glad you asked! In the current environment, the number of opportunities can be dizzying and deciding what to pursue and what to take a pass on can be difficult. This is the clear intersection of marketing/business development (a desire to secure future contracts) and resource management. The resource in question is your own time or that of your marketing department. In an ideal world, you could chase all the projects, but in reality, there are limits to what you can reasonably bid on—with the quality and success worthy of your time and reputation. There is a more detailed discussion about resource management later in the book, but a sneak peek of the topic is that your resources are not unlimited, and this is the case for all organizations, large and small. Now, here is the real secret: If you can focus in on your *what* and are disciplined in your use of resources to pursue the projects that align with the services you provide, you will be more successful. Your measure of success may be an increased win percentage, a growing backlog, or smoother cash flow, and in many respects, the metric will not matter. As a business owner, would you prefer a single satisfying scoop of ice cream you can finish, or a sundae that will be left melting on the table?

Stay In Your Lane

This is directly connected with the idea of having a clear understanding of your *what*. As an entrepreneur and business owner, you may be thinking you did not get into business to just do one thing. McDonald's sells more than burgers and fries. Gas stations sell more than just gas. That is true, but if a gas station had no gas, would you go out of your way to stop there for washer fluid, gum, cigarettes, or lottery tickets? While these companies have expanded their offerings, they first had to perfect the delivery of their core businesses. In the movie *The Founder*, about McDonald's, Ray Kroc (portrayed by Michael Keaton) did not worry about anything other than replicating the process the McDonald brothers used to operate a single restaurant. Until he understood the process and the rationale for the kitchen setup, he knew opening another location would not be successful. A further illustration of this was his visit to one of the franchises that took it upon itself to sell hot dogs and fried chicken—definitely crashing up against the guardrails of the standard burger and fries concept. His anger was apparent and he set out to put the franchise back on the path to focusing on its core offering. It is hard to stay in your lane, and I know this from personal experience. The RFP comes across your email and you start to think about preparing a proposal. You don't really provide 100 percent of the services the agency is looking to procure, but maybe you can just figure it out...

Sound familiar?

We live in an age of specialization, and one in which you can be very successful in an industry niche. I am continually amazed by the stories of businesses that have grown around the ability to be disciplined and not bounce between the guardrails. I'll give you an example.

Diego is an electrical contractor who has built his business to the point that he has administrative staff and a marketing director who filters through advertised opportunities. When I met with Diego and the marketing director, I asked about the projects they had won, their clients, and their ideal project. At the time, I assumed an electrical contractor is just that, an electrical contractor. Boy, was I wrong. They explained that within their trade they had developed a

reputation for successfully delivering expensive pieces of equipment with long lead times that are critical to the success of projects from technical and schedule perspectives. "So, you don't actually do electrical work?" They both smiled and almost in unison said "We can, but we leave that to others. We make a lot of money doing what we do."

It was clear to me then there has to be a very good reason to go outside your specialty because risks increase, profits will likely drop, and your stress level will rise as you venture outside your comfort zone. My daughter Sophie has a postcard on her wall that says "Life begins at the end of your comfort zone," and while I generally agree with that in respect to personal pursuits, with professional endeavors, the risks often outweigh any potential benefits. The purpose of a business is to make money or increase owner wealth, and if you can figure out how to do that without pushing the boundaries of your lane, do it. This is predicated on the understanding of the industry and knowledge that your specialty will likely remain in demand. There is an added benefit to staying in your lane *and* keeping a robust network of other contractors. When the call comes and it's not something you really do, you have the opportunity to refer the business to a trusted company. You will have made both the client and the other company happy and created goodwill with both and you have not spent a single dime to do it.

Managing Your Sales Funnel

When I talk to business owners about the projects and clients they are pursuing, far too often I get a laundry list of companies, clients, and agencies that sometimes looks like a bowl of alphabet soup. There is a reason we refer to successful efforts as being "on target"—there was hunting, aiming, and firing involved. However, a rich hunting environment is not necessarily about volume, but about having your business development efforts targeted and dialed in on who is buying what you are selling.

I worked with Nick for several months as his company was completing a design project for a transportation agency. The agency was primarily involved with railroads and commuter facilities, but as a one-off project, his firm was hired to design a training facility. As we talked about his marketing efforts, he mentioned how much he enjoyed the project and planned on dedicating more of his time to further develop the relationship with the agency. I stopped him after a few minutes and asked about the frequency with which the agency awarded contracts for his specialty— architectural design. "Well, I don't really know," was his honest response. Nick's experience designing buildings was a mismatch for the vast majority of work the agency awarded; he had been fortunate to land the contract he was wrapping up. We then discussed where his target-rich environment would likely be found. His target-rich environment was with agencies that are focused on buildings—universities, hospitals, housing authorities, and school systems.

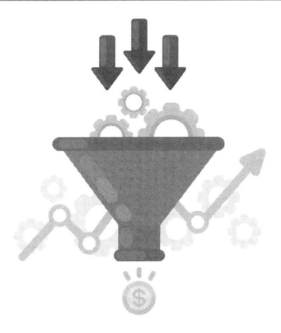

How are you filling *your* sales funnel? When we think about a sales funnel, we are thinking about all the opportunities you are considering and pursuing. A funnel, wide at the top and narrow at the bottom, is a metaphor for the fact that you will only win a certain percentage of the work you chase—in order to have the amount of work you desire at the bottom of the funnel you need a whole lot more going into the top. Once you know what you are looking for, you have to figure out where to find the opportunities. These days, the answer is literally at your fingertips, since nearly all projects in the public sector must be publicly advertised. In many cases, there are websites that consolidate those opportunities and provide the ability to filter them to the specifics of your company; they will even send you email alerts when an appropriate project gets listed. There are also private sites that operate on a subscription basis that will send alerts and provide visibility for your company.

Is that all you need to do? No, it's just one part of the equation. You will still need to attend industry meetings and project presentations, interact with potential teaming partners, create some Google alerts, and read the industry news (online, print, and social media) to get a fuller view of the potential projects to throw into the top of the funnel.

Even before you think about responding to an RFP or RFQ, it is critical to understand the nature of the work different agencies and potential clients complete. We talked earlier about managing your resources—your time, effort, and money—and this becomes a relevant issue when it comes to chasing potential projects, because you don't have enough of any resource to pursue everything. As the knight in *Indiana Jones and the Last Crusade* presciently said, "Choose wisely." Your goal is to fill the funnel with the right kinds of opportunities and leads so the work that drops out of the bottom is targeted and relevant, and puts you on the path to success and growth.

It's All About Relationships

There are times when this concept becomes a difficult sell with my clients, especially as it relates to contracts in the public sector. The overwhelming assumption is always that decisions are based on pure costs—the lowest bidder gets the job. In reality, most documents indicate the project will be awarded to the "lowest *responsible* bidder," which means agencies have latitude to reject the lowest bid if they have reason to believe the bidder cannot complete the project for the quoted price. They can reject bids for many reasons if they have concerns about integrity, past performance, quality of subcontractors, etc. Does that mean developing a relationship with agency staff alone will give you a leg up in the bidding process? No, but a relationship with agency staff can lead to referrals, discretionary projects that do not require public bidding, or a heads-up about things that may be on the horizon in the industry.

As you think about your target agencies or companies and past performance with them, the relationships you have developed with their project managers can be instrumental in winning additional work, assuming you are competitively bidding the project. What is the value of a good evaluation and recommendation from an insider at an agency? Priceless. Let's face it: no agency or contracting company expects everything to go perfectly all the time. The companies that keep their clients informed and up-to-date on progress (good and bad) in a proactive, transparent manner build up a bank account of trust that, when things go badly, can be drawn from to mitigate the situation. Over time, those client relationships become critical in winning more work, because clients like to award projects to companies they know and trust.

Building relationships throughout your professional life is more than collecting business cards and connecting on LinkedIn; relationships are two-way streets paved with honesty, good intentions, and generosity. Building relationships can often be even more relevant if you are pursuing projects as a subcontractor. Say you have decided to stay in your niche and grow as a preferred vendor to a larger firm. This means you want to be the first person called when there is a need for your particular specialty and pure costs will not be weighed as heavily as they might if you are a prime contract holder. What are the criteria going to be in this situation? Previous experience working with the company, a track record delivering similar work, qualified staff, competitive costs? Yes, to all of the above.

Here is a secret—well, not so much a secret, but something often unrecognized: many public agencies have specific small business programs designed to provide an entree into the agency without competing against larger, more established companies. You still have to compete in most cases, but you are competing against similarly-sized companies, and there is even greater discretion in the awarding of contracts. Yes, there are financial limits to the awards, but the relationship you can develop with the agency staff puts you in a position of advantage, and sometimes, with the ability to craft your own scope of work. If you have identified a potential problem and can help solve it within the limits of the program, your likelihood of performing the work increases. Finding the opportunities requires two things: dedication and relationships.

Here are just a few relationships that will be important to your marketing and business development efforts:

 Current clients

 Previous clients (agencies and prime contractors)

 Subcontractors and subconsultants

 Vendors

 Competitors (you never know when an opportunity to collaborate will arise)

 Colleagues in related fields

 Target agencies and companies

Networking

When I hear the word *networking*, I get an uneasy feeling in the pit of my stomach. For me, going to a networking event where I likely won't know anybody seems about as much fun as getting a root canal. For others, this may be akin to being a kid in a candy store. Wherever you land on the spectrum between "oh no!" and "bring it on," networking is an important part of what you need to do as a business owner, regardless of the business you are in. The important thing to remember is you are not there just for the free food or the chance to avoid rush hour. What is it you want to get out of the networking event? What do you want to learn? Who would you like to meet?

Kate's company asked her to represent the firm at an industry conference. She sat at the table in the expo and talked to attendees about the company, its needs, and how it operated when it came to working with subs. Kate spoke to tons of people, but observed something interesting. "The people who were really interested in working with us took the time to wait, even if I was in the middle of a conversation, to make a connection. One person started taking notes on the back of my business card." The others? "They would see me in a conversation and would stick a business card in my hand and keep walking. No waiting, no conversation, no connection."

As I mentioned previously, adages can be well-worn sayings that continue to hold resonance and value. In this context, there are two that always seem to ring true, irrespective of your line of business, position, or goal in life—and I've already used them:

 People like to do business with people they know and trust.

 You don't get a second chance to make a good first impression.

So, when you are thinking about the next industry mixer or outreach event, keep these in mind because you don't want a reputation as the person wallpapering the place with business cards but not taking the opportunity for real conversations. It's OK to be nervous, but it's not OK to appear rude or uninterested.

Presenting Yourself Online And In Print

It sometimes feels like everyone wants to be the next Instagram influencer or YouTube darling; the siren song of the internet and social media can be intoxicating. Have you had the experience of finding a company online that has a great-looking website but miserable customer service? Or a company that advertises a great offer, but when you call, there are all sorts of fine print that excludes most from exercising the opportunity? Me, too.

A website can be a great marketing tool, and increasingly, the first bar a company needs to meet when it comes to establishing credibility. In fact, a good website—well-designed, clean, clear in purpose and services—can make you look bigger, more successful, and more accomplished than you are in reality. That's OK as long as you don't misrepresent your *what*, your experience, or your expertise. As a small business owner in the construction industry, I generally advocate a simple website with the following pages:

 Landing Page

 About Us

 Projects

 Clients

 Contact (and in fact, your contact information should be on every page of your website)

Give it some color, photos, testimonials, a logo, and easy-to-read text. Beyond that, I don't recommend spending a lot of money or time on it, but find someone who can make sure it accurately reflects who you are, what you do, and how you bring value to your clients—unless you happen to love coding websites, though it will pull resources (your time) away from working on your business. Is a potential client going to hire you just off your website? Perhaps if you sell a product, but when it comes to services, most (if not all) clients will want to meet you in person and ensure you are who you claim to be. Again, we are really talking about establishing some baseline credibility, and it is astonishing to me how many companies and agencies assume the worst in the absence of a website. More and more, a website is a *need to have*, not a *nice to have*.

There are other online presences to consider, and I'm not talking about social media like Facebook, LinkedIn, and Instagram, though I'll get to that shortly. If you are in a position where you want to work as a subcontractor or subconsultant, how do you expect the primes to find you beyond doing a Google search that may not return your company website until the third, eighth, or even fifteenth page of results? For work in the public sector, find the registries for companies like yours through your local municipality or state.

Where I live in New York, there are registries run by New York State and New York City that provide the opportunity to identify the type of work you do, whether that is a construction trade, professional service, product, or consulting offering. This is particularly important for companies with some type of certification status as an MBE, WBE, DBE, or SDVOB. Certification is important and discussed in the next section. You have to make it easy for larger companies to find you and for them to have a good understanding of your services that match their project needs. In addition to the government-run sites that provide information about projects being advertised, there are also private subscription-based sites providing similar opportunities and generally work with companies to ensure the profiles are accurate, searchable, and contain appropriate keywords.

Certification Is Important To The Private Sector, Too

The value of certification is hard to quantify because it does not provide a guarantee you will be awarded any work. All certification does is unlock the door to opportunities, and it is your responsibility to open the door, step inside, and find the right opportunities to highlight your value proposition. I come at this with some experience as a WBE; my wife and I got her company certified years ago and I can tell you that there have been opportunities for us, not because of the certification but because of the quality of our work. The agency staff's eyes light up when they learn that they can take credit for the contract they award. In the public sector, certifications generally fall into four categories; there are too many certifying agencies to list them all, but the main certifications are:

 Minority Business Enterprise (MBE)

 Women's Business Enterprise (WBE)

 Disadvantaged Business Enterprise (DBE)

 Service-Disabled Veteran-Owned Business (SDVOB)

With most public procurements, advertising agencies establish goals for particular projects, but do not determine how to meet that goal—they leave that to prime contract holders. Here's the tricky part: guidelines and the level of importance placed on diversity and inclusion vary from state to state.

For the most part, DBE certification includes MBE and WBE firms, but applies to projects with federal funding. In most cases, any federal funding—even $1—will necessitate the use of DBEs, and the percentages will vary for locally funded projects. The other wrinkle to DBE certification is that even though it is a federal certification, each state has its own process. So, if you are DBE-certified in California, that does not give you certification in Nevada, right next door. Why is that important? With all certifications, prime contract holders can only take credit for work awarded to companies that are certified to perform that specific work category—pending certification does not count.

Jack is the owner of a small company specializing in corporate fit outs that has been slowly making the transition to public agency projects. At first, he worked as a subcontractor doing interior construction—framing, sheetrock, painting, tiling, etc.—when he got a call from a larger general contractor looking for his company to take a major role in an upcoming project. He was excited when I spoke to him because the project would likely bring in over $1 million in revenue over the next six months. He was going on and on about the work and all the different elements, which included new lighting, electrical services, and bathrooms. Jack and I worked together to get his companied certified, but I knew he wasn't certified for the electrical and plumbing work;

he had overlooked that when he agreed to the project. It created a challenge for him, the general contractor, and the agency. The GC and agency expected to get credit for the $1 million subcontract with an MBE. He still completed the project, but had to bring in other companies to do the work he was not certified to perform, reducing his share of the project. He took on greater responsibility and oversight, which eroded his net profit, but he delivered the project on time and on budget. It was a good lesson for Jack about understanding the rules and regulations, and their real-world implications.

MBE, WBE, and SDVOB certifications become hyper local, so managing them is critical as you begin to zero in on your target agencies. For example, in New York there is certification for New York City and New York State, and some of the New York City agencies even have their own certification procedures. The advice I give to any firm thinking about getting certified is to track certifications carefully, because if they lapse, you could easily find yourself back at square one. The process is involved and time-consuming, and carries many, many, many document requirements. The good part is that many of the documents are common to all applications (e.g., personal and corporate tax returns, financial statements, references, and corporate documents) so once you have compiled them, keep them.

My experience helping companies through the certification process includes the following recommendations:

Organize. Create an organized filing system for the paper—not a shoebox in the corner. In places where you still need to submit the application in a paper format, make it easy for the reviewer to go through the documentation. Provide a table of contents, and if there is something "not applicable" to your company, provide a letter indicating that situation.

Scan. Scan the documents and save them on your computer. If something gets lost, you want to easily retrieve the information for the certifying agency.

Track. Track your expiration dates. Most agencies certify for three to five years and you will likely be contacted as the expiration approaches, but not always. A simple spreadsheet will do the trick.

Start early. Certification will almost always take longer than you expect. If your application is pending and you have an opportunity that relies upon certification, some agencies will expedite the review, but you can't count on that.

Micro purchasing can be a profitable way to build your company as a certified business. In many locales, an emphasis has been placed on awarding contracts to smaller companies that are certified. How micro is micro? Well, as of this writing, New York State agencies can award contracts of up to $200,000 (though limits are expected to increase) without a full RFP process, although you will be competing with comparable companies. New York City agencies have the latitude to award contracts up to $150,000. This works out well for those agencies because the contracting process becomes less cumbersome and the projects tend to be shorter in duration. Some departments within the agencies will have "p-card" privileges where they can procure goods and services for, in some cases, upward of $25,000. The important thing to remember is these programs are generally designed for certified companies; you need to know about them so you can ask about them. Many of the agencies call the programs by different names—Discretionary Procurement, Small Business Procurement, Diversity Procurement Programs—but they mostly operate in a similar manner. I can imagine you thinking, "OK, what's the catch?" The catch is you have to deliver that work with the same quality and professionalism as any other project.

For a time, I managed a small business program, and we not only provided coaching and consulting but also the opportunity to bid on smaller contracts that a growing company could handle.

Sue, a small business owner in the program, came into my office one day and asked when she would be given a project. After all, her company was certified and her services were in line with the agency's needs. I gently explained to her that certification was not a golden ticket or a guarantee. The agency does not give work to vendors; vendors have to earn the opportunity to deliver a project. We had a long conversation about strategy, approach, marketing, and expectations. I left her with the following guidance in interacting with agencies: you have to be competent, qualified, responsive, and responsible, and oh yeah, "I also happen to be certified."

The agencies and prime contract holders want the certification, but the first four are the primary determinants.

And The Measure Of Effective Marketing Is . . .

In the same way I advocate tracking your work in progress (WIP) and your completed projects, the first step in the process should be tracking the work you are bidding and who you are bidding with (prime contractor and agency). This lets you get a better view of which clients and agencies have proven to be fruitful and which have been duds. It's important to understand there can be a little bait and switch in the industry, and sometimes a prime contractor will shop for an estimate and then ask a preferred subcontractor to do the work for that price. By tracking the bids you prepare, that dynamic will show up, affording you the opportunity for a more direct conversation the next time one of those contractors calls.

A word of caution about conversion rates: stuff happens. Projects get cancelled, projects are scaled back, and projects get delayed or the like—and it likely has nothing to do with you. But asking the right questions (using those refined communications tools) will not only get you the information you need, but highlight you and your company in a professional and responsible way (enhancing your personal and corporate brands). Trust me when I tell you the big primes know what they spend on marketing, their return on investment, and their conversion rates, and they have a system for deciding what projects to pursue. If you want to be like them, you need to implement the same kind of rigor in using your marketing tools.

4X4 IN MARKETING

So, what does 4x4 performance look like as it pertains to marketing?

 Competence comes down to having a very-well-refined idea of what you do, how you do it, and the value you bring to potential clients. Understand your lane and how to find the targeted and appropriate opportunities. Qualified firms can demonstrate past performance and articulate the value proposition with respect to business development activities.

Qualification also includes having the necessary business intelligence, marketing materials, and references to establish your ability and credibility to deliver a project successfully.

 Responsiveness takes on a whole range of competencies, but in the marketing and business development realm, it means you understand deadlines and can meet them. A proposal due on March 15 by 3 p.m. must be submitted by that date and time; March 15 at 5 p.m. is unacceptable. The same goes for working with a prime consultant or contractor. Ask the right questions— what do you need from me and by when?

 Last, *responsible* marketing includes not promising services you can't deliver during conversations you have with potential clients. As William Shakespeare famously wrote: "To thine own self be true." Those are words to live by as you market yourself and your company. The 4x4 performance approach will allow you to leverage the certifications you may have, but the first four should be considered the price of admission to the procurement party.

CORNERSTONE QUESTIONS TO SUPPORT YOUR SUCCESS:

- What does your marketing material say about you? How can you determine if it resonates with your clients?

- How well can you articulate what you do and don't do?

- What would it feel like to fill your sales funnel with the right opportunities and have an abundance of work? What challenges would that present to you and your company? How might you address those challenges?

- What other opportunities are available to further leverage your certification? If you are eligible but not yet certified, what support would you need to secure your certification?

CHAPTER 9

Your Human Resources Tools: Take A People-First Approach

The range of issues that fall into the very broad category of human resources can be dizzying, and in many cases, are the most challenging part of owning a business. It seems the length of tenure for staff keeps getting shorter and shorter as the industry continues to pump out increasingly larger capital programs. There was a time when hiring managers would look at interviewees disapprovingly if they saw a work history of jumping from company to company every three to five years. Much of that has changed, though there are still some old-school companies that frown on the idea of moving for projects and more responsibility.

Invariably, human resources can be challenging because the process involves people, emotions, ever-changing needs and circumstances, and different perspectives and attitudes. As a small business owner, there is some value to replicating, as best as possible, the practices employed by larger organizations. My advice when it relates to building like the big primes is *don't reinvent the wheel*. There are a lot of resources available online, from colleagues in the

"YOU HAVING A HARD TIME
FINDING QUALIFIED WORKERS?"

industry, clients, and government agencies like the Small Business Administration. While there can be a lot of stress associated with human resources, it can be very rewarding when you use the right tools to grow your company with the right people.

Hire For Fit, Teach The Rest

As I sit at my desk writing this, the unemployment rate sits below 4 percent, which by most measures, means most people who want a job likely have a job. What does that mean for you? It means you have to be creative and flexible regarding your hiring process and identifying staff for your company. The first step in the process is really determining what your needs are—short term and critical to growth, medium term for anticipated projects, and longer term to accommodate planned growth.

Daniela came to me with a desperate need for an estimator to help complete proposals for a variety of projects she had been invited to bid on from past clients. She was stretched to her limit and needed support in doing takeoffs from the plans. As we spoke over coffee and picked apart her most pressing needs, we developed a plan to address the immediate situation and her longer-term needs. She ultimately reached out to another contractor with whom she had developed a relationship, and was able to tap into the excess capacity of its estimator. In reality, Daniela

needed more than a pure estimator—she needed someone who could handle a variety of tasks, but she did not have the ability to take on the expense of a full-time employee until some new work materialized. So, what could she do in the medium term? We came up with a creative solution. Daniela contacted the local community college that offered a two-year degree in construction technology. She found a bright energetic student to work variable hours while still in school who was a whiz with computers, eager to learn, and was hoping it might turn into a full-time job after graduation. It ended up being a great match and Daniela made her a permanent job offer six months later.

Hiring full-time staff is one of the most daunting challenges I hear from clients—from advertising, recruiting, interviewing, and onboarding to getting over the fear of needing to make payroll every week. Let's talk about a creative approach to meeting some needs, perhaps before you are ready, have a demonstrated need, or are still dealing with some apprehension. Community colleges and universities are a tremendous source of smart and capable options for part-time staff who can, hopefully, become full-time employees when you are both ready to make that commitment. There are any number of advantages to exploring this route for needed talent, but the cost factor alone makes this an attractive option. College students will not have the same salary demands as graduates looking for full-time positions. Additionally, you can often bring on interns as 1099 employees as opposed to W-2 status, but I recommend a conversation with your attorney or accountant about the various approaches.

Flexibility is key. A college intern is not likely interested in a forty-hour per week position, and that would not necessarily fit with your current needs. With the right match, an agreement about the number of hours per week and the changing nature of the workload can make for a successful arrangement and relationship. Also, technology is always changing and college students tend to be on the forefront of those changes; many grew up having to self-teach. The adaptability to particular software programs will generally lead to a much shorter learning curve than might be expected from a more seasoned candidate.

College career officers tend to be willing partners and are happy to help you find what you need. They understand this is a win-win-win situation. The student wins by securing a position while in school to gain some real-world experience. The school wins because it can tout its ability to place students and bring additional employers into its sphere. You win by getting the talent you need without all the commitment or breaking the bank.

When it comes to interviewing, having been on both sides of the desk in the process, I can appreciate the stress for each of the participants. Once candidates meet the basic qualifications, I often use the "lunchroom test" to make decisions about moving them forward to the next step in the process. Considering we often spend more hours a week at work with our coworkers and employees than we do with our families, I like to think about having lunch with a candidate every day. Can I see myself sharing meals with this person? Do our styles mesh? This can often be a helpful lens to look through in evaluating candidates—assuming they already meet the basic needs of the position and you have confidence in their ability to perform and deliver.

In the context of diversity, the only caveat is to be aware of your own inherent biases, and we all have them. It may be more comfortable to hire someone who looks and sounds like you, but there is a tremendous likelihood you will lose out on some awesome talent if that is your measuring stick. Diversity does not just mean age, gender, or ethnicity. The beauty of diversity is about the melding of thought processes, mindsets, and perspectives that lead to enhanced decision-making, more creative solutions, and better outcomes. Don't just ask yourself about a candidate, "is she a culture fit?" Ask yourself, "is she a culture *add*?" You want to hire people who can both fit into and add to your team and business.

What Gets Measured Gets Managed

As a manager, you may dread performance reviews. They can seem time-consuming, highlight a lack of definition around the employees' roles and responsibilities, or feel like a *nice to have* rather than a critical measurement tool. Surprisingly, there are a lot of big companies that do not conduct performance reviews, so this is an area where even a small company can outperform the big players. (Sometimes you don't want to build like the big primes unless they are operating in a way worth emulating.)

James had experienced financial success and business growth over the previous year, and brought on a new project manager and field staff. He expressed reservations about the performance of his new PM. As we spoke, I asked him, "Are his projects on time and on budget?" to which he nodded approvingly. "Is the client happy with his approach and communications?" Another approving nod. "Does his staff respect him and respond to his requests?" Yes, of course. "So, James, what seems to be the problem?" It turns

out there was an expectation that his new PM would help with the preparation of proposals and estimates, but he had yet to take the initiative to pitch in.

So what was the issue? These expectations were never formally included in the job description, nor had there been explicit conversations about the need for the PM's assistance in tasks beyond the management of projects. In this case, the PM's performance (or perceived lack of performance) could be chalked up to James's lack of clarity about the expectations of the job, In fact, the PM was doing an excellent job delivering on the tasks for which he was hired, and James had to own his role here. He couldn't reasonably expect an employee to do a job he didn't know he was supposed to be doing!

As your team begins to grow, consider the following:

Create basic job descriptions for all categories of positions within the company. Once you have them and you feel comfortable they cover the basics, you can tailor them for individuals who may be expected to take on additional responsibilities. If you do not feel comfortable doing this, I recommend you reach out to colleagues who may be willing to share job descriptions, or start with an online job posting that reasonably covers the role.

Once the roles and responsibilities have been documented, share them with your staff so they have a clear sense of what you expect of them. Give them the opportunity to weigh in and offer comments on what tasks they complete that may not be explicitly spelled out.

Every employee is entitled to a formal conversation about performance at least once a year, but I do not recommend you limit your conversations to the formal discussion. The cost to correct defects in construction when identified after completion is 150 times greater than with early intervention. Similarly, performance issues identified and addressed early are much easier to correct when they are minor. Think "early and often" when it comes to giving performance feedback.

Self-evaluations are a great way to get a sense of how employees view their own performance. A word of caution—most employees will cast their performance as excellent and better than their peers. Don't discount everything they say, but try to include questions that are concrete, quantifiable, and verifiable.

If you want your employees to be open and responsive to receiving feedback from you about their performance, you need to model that you are open and responsive to receiving feedback from them as well. Feedback is a two-way street, and you can create a culture of continuous improvement if you're willing to be a part of the solution.

I worked for a company for a number of years that had a rigorous performance evaluation process, and in that time, I had the same manager for three consecutive years. Each April, as we were discussing other items, he would casually slide my evaluation across his desk and say, "Oh, by the way, I need you to sign this." Each year, I read his evaluation of my performance and quickly signed on the last page. There were no surprises, no corrections needed, and no inaccuracies. We had open and honest lines of communication, and there had been conversations throughout the year about my performance, as well as opportunities for me to provide feedback to him. Our situation may have been more unusual than that of some others on the team, but I would encourage you to foster a feeling of openness, where the formal conversation is not fraught with undue anxiety and can be used as a jumping off point for a discussion about personal and professional development.

Know What Makes Your Employees Tick

My favorite course in graduate school, and the one I discuss more than any other, was organizational behavior. At a very basic level, organizational behavior digs into what motivates employees to work long hours, travel long distances, and do physically and/or cognitively taxing work. Depending on where your offices or projects are located, you may have staff that travel in excess of two hours each way to get to work. How you keep them engaged and productive is all covered in the course on organizational behavior—as well as a host of other interesting and useful concepts. The most surprising concept I learned was that motivation rarely has anything to do with the digits on employees' paychecks, assuming they are being paid fairly and can cover their basic expenses. Once I became a team leader, manager, and supervisor, this idea became even clearer and relevant.

Katerina was concerned she would lose out on good candidates to larger companies because they were paying $5,000 more per year than she could afford to offer. We talked about the benefits (beyond health insurance, vacation, sick days, etc.) that her company could provide to potential candidates, as well as expanded roles. As she mulled it over, she came up with a whole range of benefits that could put her offer ahead of the big companies despite a lower (but competitive) salary. For the less senior staff she was looking to recruit, the size of her company meant greater responsibility and access to clients more quickly than in a larger, more structured company. The open-door policy Katerina had created resulted in a mentoring environment, featuring ongoing discussions about the business, career path, and problem-solving. And, perhaps most appreciated by the staff were the monthly happy hours and Summer Fridays, which gave employees the option of adjusting their schedules from Memorial Day to Labor Day so they could have three-day weekends twice per month. By reframing *her offers with nonmonetary benefits, Kate was able to attract employees who fit the culture, could do the job, and would hopefully see her company as a place to grow a career.*

While understanding what motivates employees is important, so is the ability to manage staff, communicate clearly, and develop a flexible style to work with a variety of personalities and circumstances. After all, recruiting and onboarding are just a small piece of getting maximum value and productivity from your employees. In many respects, and I have found this throughout my career, managing staff, balancing their needs, and keeping employees focused takes a lot of energy, and that does not begin to consider the work associated with delegating tasks, mentoring, coaching, and advising. A chapter follows on coaching, mentoring, and the difference between them, and why that is important to a business owner. When you are starting to think about the culture you want to create and benefits you are offering to employees, here are a few ideas to consider:

Rome was not built in a day, and the culture of your company will also take some time to develop. Be patient and think about the kind of environment you'd like to have for you and your staff before you just start trying to create it in a piecemeal fashion. As you begin thinking about different options, evaluate whether they are practical or reasonable. As a trade contractor, your busy season will likely begin in March and run through October or November, so Summer Fridays are not going to be workable for you or your clients, but there are other ways to engage your employees.

Nonmonetary benefits will still have hard and soft costs. The costs may be based on your time talking to an employee about a career path, or the longer time to complete a project through collaboration and consensus building. It will be important to evaluate the costs and benefits of any solution or approach prior to implementation What are the opportunity costs associated with spending time with your team? What else might you be doing and would it be more valuable? In the allocation of your time, it is often just as valuable to talk to your staff instead of returning an email or having coffee with a potential teaming partner. Are there benefits in engaging your employees? Without a doubt, as long as you are conscious of the time and the other priorities on your plate.

You have two ears and one mouth—listen twice as much as you speak. Invariably, if you really listen to your employees, vendors, and clients, they will provide the early warning signs of potential trouble. In addition to listening to your employees, be curious and ask them questions about themselves, including their goals and aspirations, and solicit their ideas for ways to improve the company or culture.

Respect the research—even if it seems counterintuitive. Research shows once you meet a person's basic financial needs, motivating factors include liking the people you work with, recognition, developing expertise, having a sense of purpose, being offered growth opportunities, having autonomy over tasks, and flexibility. If you can incorporate some or all of these motivators—and the many more you can find by doing your own research—the likelihood of attracting and maintaining quality employees will increase.

Is it easy to create the right balance and culture? No it isn't, especially with industries like ours that are not particularly known for workplace innovation. You are not Google or Amazon with sleep pods, ping pong tables, or elaborate cafeterias, and you would not necessarily offer them even if you could. However, your employees are your most valuable asset and the benefits you offer can pay dividends for years to come as your company grows and matures.

"For those of you going off to work, today's forecast calls for 8 to 10 inches of paperwork...."

"Where's Your Paperwork?"

By far, that is one of my family's favorite quotes by Roz from the Pixar movie *Monsters, Inc.* As a business owner, this is an important question to ask, and in our increasingly digital world, it really goes to your ability to put your hands on important documents. What paperwork are we talking about here? From a human resources perspective, this will include résumés, performance reviews, insurance enrollment forms, 401(k) documents, job descriptions, interview notes, and company policies and procedures. A few thoughts on filing your paperwork—don't rely just on email systems and the attachments as a substitute for saving documents. This seems to be the default approach with many business owners I talk to and consult with.

Susan had recently hired four new employees, bringing her overall staff to fifteen, and she anticipated the need for at least another two or three employees before the end of the year. She complained to me that each new employee and person she interviewed "heard what they wanted to hear" and it was causing some concerns for her about everyone working off the same playbook. I asked her what she gave potential employees along with the offer letter. Unfortunately, that was all she gave them, along with a brief description of benefits—fifteen days PTO, health insurance, and access to a 401(k) plan. While Susan had

a strong, ethical perspective and only hired employees who felt the same way, there was no explicit explanation about a code of conduct, policies regarding use of personal leave, use of company equipment, or use of personal phones during the workday. We found some good resources and modified them for her company and then gave her new employee handbook to her attorney to review. The "playbook" was distributed to all employees and was provided to all interviewees, which led to a level playing field.

My wife Deborah, a small business owner, has often said that the only thing standing between her and everything she's ever wanted is paperwork. I don't know too many people who get excited about completing paperwork, whether it relates to invoicing, monthly reports, performance reviews, prequalification packages, or insurance, but the ability to accurately document situations, particularly as it relates to human resources, can provide the protection you need. An area where this paperwork becomes critically important is the documentation of employee behavior, especially if you are noticing negative patterns like excessive absences, routine lateness, or disregarding management requests. As a manager or business owner, the most challenging conversation you will have with an employee will include some version of "we no longer have a place for you here," which can have any number of consequences for your company, including getting sued for wrongful termination or paying unemployment benefits. Hopefully, you don't find yourself in that position, but if you do and you sit across the table from your attorney, the question will come—where's your paperwork?

Develop a consistent approach across all of human resources. Standard documents will serve your company exceedingly well for all phases of human resources, including job applications, job descriptions, performance assessments, and employee handbooks. This will standardize your human resource function without even having a human resource department.

Make sure you know where the documents are, whether in a file drawer or the cloud. Create a filing system to store and manage all the paper. Even better, scan and electronically file the information so you have access at a moment's notice.

Let them know where they stand. Communication with employees about performance is essential to ensure expectations are known and met, and that employees are aware of any performance issues. Measures can be taken to correct any issues; and in the event an employee has to be terminated, the situation will be fully documented.

Don't go it alone. Consult with professionals as you are preparing to issue any official company rules and regulations to protect your company and guard against any unintended consequences. While there are many free templates available, use a professional to customize them to your needs and protect your company.

What About Labor Unions?

To paraphrase Hamlet: "To join or not to join, that is the question." And what a decision it is for a trade contractor! In many respects, the answer to the question really rests on a number of circumstances, including your company goals (revenue), client base (sales), type of projects (public sector or private), and openness to running your business with a different operating model. Union affiliation is not the only approach to some projects; there are nonunion set asides and project labor agreements (PLAs) that become a hybrid approach and offer contractors the opportunity to dip their toes in the union water. Affiliating with a union is not the only tool to facilitate growth, but it can be the fuel to build the fire you have already kindled.

Chris has been working for public agencies and has typically found himself as a prime contractor for smaller projects. Along the way, there has been a lot of interaction with the union that covers his core work, but he has resisted its overtures at affiliation. In general, it has never been a significant impediment to growth, but the relationship can be challenging, since the union believes any work from the agencies should fall into its sphere of influence. He was able to push back, with the help of the agency staff, to remain a

nonunion contractor. Recently, Chris was approached by a large prime contractor that is a union contractor. The prime was very interested in awarding a significant subcontract and created a PLA for Chris and the other subcontractors that worked for all parties. The union got its dues; the prime got its preferred subcontractors; and Chris got a new contract and started a new, and hopefully, profitable relationship.

When I talk to many of my clients, they are nervous, apprehensive, or scared of joining a union because the perception is once they do, they will relinquish control of their company. In many municipalities, the public works projects are already designated as prevailing wage projects where the wages—by trade and job title—have been set as a way to ensure a fair wage for craft labor and level the playing field among bidders. For contractors that are already paying prevailing wages, the transition to union rates is actually quite small. In New York, for example, the difference between the two rates is only a few dollars per hour. So, you should join the union, right? Maybe. As previously mentioned, there are ways to gain access to the types of projects that will help you grow without joining a trade union, but the vast majority of prime contractors completing public projects are union contractors. While there may be some reservations about affiliating with a particular union, there are a few aspects to consider.

Let the unions do their part. Remember the discussion about paperwork? A significant component of completing a construction project, and often an impediment to success, is the ability to submit accurate and timely invoices. With any public project, the client is going to require a certified payroll register that details all payroll and benefits paid to ensure either prevailing or union wages have been accurately paid. If you are a union contractor, payroll and benefits get paid through the local union, which can provide the necessary payroll register.

From a business operations perspective, joining a union will alleviate the need for administrative staff to generate your payroll, manage benefits programs, and recruit staff. There will still be administrative activities remaining with your company, but you can take those three off your plate.

Labor will be available at the end of a phone call. As a small and growing contractor, you likely are not going to get the cream of the union crop, but you can be assured of trained and competent staff. My advice is to flatten out your workflow to the point where you can maintain your core staff throughout the year.

Meet with and get to know local union representatives. In most cases, the unions are receptive to growing companies and will recognize any hesitations. Talk to your prime contractors and agency contacts about their interactions with the union and develop a full range of questions you would need to have answered before signing on the bottom line. Have your attorney review the union agreement so you fully understand the guidelines and requirements.

4X4 IN HUMAN RESOURCES

What does it mean to be a 4x4 performer as it pertains to your company's human resources?

 Competent contractors figure out a way to identify, recruit, and hire good staff to facilitate the completion of their projects. Competency also includes the ability to effectively manage employee performance and address deficiencies as early as possible.

 Qualified contractors maintain staff that have the requisite skill set to do the job and do it right. Training and upgrading of skills should be viewed as an investment in your employees' growth and advancement toward your company goals.

 Responsive contractors have their ear to the ground and listen for any problems that may be on the horizon. In many respects, managing people and diverse personalities can lead to a festering situation if left alone. Listen to your team, your clients, and your colleagues for any challenging dynamics that will not keep everyone on track and moving in sync.

Responsible contractors not only manage people and projects, but also the process, which for human resources is often related to providing certified payroll, benefits, and fostering relationships with local trade unions.

"I BET WE COULD HAVE PUT YOU TOGETHER
IF WE'D GONE THROUGH ALL THE
KING'S UNION APPRENTICE PROGRAMS."

CORNERSTONE QUESTIONS TO SUPPORT YOUR SUCCESS:

■ What three words would your employees currently use to describe their work environment? What three words would you want them to use six months from now?

■ What are the factors that are impacting your ability to attract and retain employees? What does your interview and onboarding process look like? Your performance review process? Your exit interview process?

■ How might you create a more diverse and inclusive culture and what would the impact be on attracting talent?

■ If you had access to more qualified labor, what might be possible for you and your company?

■ How are you currently engaging your employees and supporting their professional development?

CHAPTER 10

Coaching, Mentoring, And Consulting: Don't Go It Alone

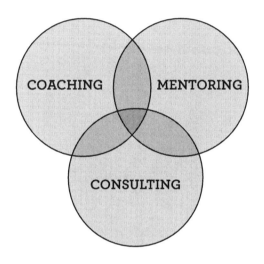

To win the board game of Trivial Pursuit, you have to fill in each of the wedges corresponding with each specific subject and also get to the middle of the board and answer a question on the subject area of your competitors' choosing. (I know this because there is a growing list of people who have sworn never to play with me ever again. What can I say? I have a mind for random sports facts, minor historical events, and arcane television references—all of which I have passed down to my son Jacob, who is a nationally-ranked sports and entertainment trivia competitor.)

At this point, you have worked your way through the hardware store and stocked your toolbox with tools from each department: finance, marketing, business operations, human resources, communications, and branding—essentially earning the bright-colored wedges. Is any one of them more important than the others? Well, you can't get to the middle of the board to try to win the game without some level of mastery in all six areas.

It is also important to remember the value of being a lifelong learner who is not satisfied meeting the basic level of mastery. As your company grows, issues will become more complex and difficult to deal with, so willingness to continue to add to your toolbox will serve you well in the long run. As your business grows and new challenges crop up, don't hesitate to pull out your toolbox and revisit these six core topics.

In addition to focusing on the six cores, this book lays out a structure of 4x4 performance upon which you can build a stable foundation. If you think about each of the elements—*competent, qualified, responsive,* and *responsible*—as the cornerstones of your business philosophy, you want to make sure they are level and plumb so you can continue building the structure of the business. The focus on 4x4 performance in these areas, equally implemented every day, will yield untold qualitative and quantitative benefits to you, your business, and your ability to meet your overall personal and professional goals.

And so, we arrive at the middle of the board for the final tools that will help you win the game: coaching, mentoring, and consulting. In my work with clients, I often wear all three hats—but they're not all the same.

Coaching, mentoring, and consulting can seem like indistinguishable concepts, but they can be viewed as a Venn diagram with overlapping circles because there are some common elements among them. The most basic and common component associated with coaching, mentoring, and consulting is centered on forward progress, clarifying goals, creating a plan to achieve them, and creating accountability for actions and results. Sometimes you will need a sounding board (coaching), sometimes advice (mentoring), and sometimes direct assistance (consulting). Knowing which kind of direction or support you need when facing a challenge is no different than selecting a tool from your toolbox.

The time will come, or has already come, when you feel pulled in fourteen different directions and are stretched to the point of snapping. This is pretty common for small business owners, as we talked about in the previous chapters, and asking for or hiring help should be considered a sign of strength.

What Is Coaching?

It is important to separate coaching into two components—internal and external. You might engage a coach to help you address personal, professional, and business goals and, as a leader and business owner, you can provide coaching to help your employees meet their own goals. Whether you're working with an external coach, or you're providing internal coaching to an employee, coaches take a similar approach: helping the client work through options and alternatives to address a situation, and then become the accountability partner for the plan moving forward. If you are feeling a little confused, think about it this way: Neither legendary UCLA basketball coach John Wooden or New York Yankees manager Joe Torre took a free throw or swung a bat, but they were able to guide their players and teams to greater results. Their ultimate goal, and that of any coach, is to support those being coached to process situations on their own and make reasoned and reasonable decisions.

If you decide to wade into the internet and start learning more about coaching, you will find every flavor and stripe of coaching—performance coaching, accountability coaching, executive coaching, life coaching, career coaching, business coaching—each with its own perspective. Not all of them will be for you, based on your needs, interests, goals, and temperament. Nevertheless, regardless of the kind of coaching, while the coach is an active partner in the process, the client does the hard work, and is responsible for advancing the process and achieving the outcomes.

(A word about language: In the context of coaching, the reference to a "client" is to the person receiving coaching as compared to a traditional view of a client as being the company or agency hiring you for a project.)

When I think about my personal outlook on coaching, as a coach and when I am being coached, there are a number of elements that rise to the top of the list in prominence and may be of help in your role as a business owner:

Goal setting. Coaching is a goal-focused (or solution-focused) approach, so the ability to elicit clear, well-defined, and emotionally engaging goals from a client is one of the most important skills for a coach to possess. The goal-setting process (the what, the how, and the speed of implementation) are all individual to the person being coached, and require that person's buy-in and commitment, so the real work of goal-setting is done not by the coach, but by the client.

Looking. The coaching process starts with looking and examining the person's perspective about a current challenge, dilemma or opportunity, not by doing something immediately or fixing it right away. This is the act of holding up the situation for reflection and studying it from all sides. This could be in relation to an employee's performance or challenges around communications. As a coach, I might ask "How is this affecting you individually and the business as a whole?" Or "What is the best possible outcome?" and "What are some solutions you haven't yet tried?"

Listening. I spend most of my time as a coach listening to my clients—actively listening. Active listening is not the same as hearing; it's being invested and involved in the conversation even if your mouth is not moving. Active listening is the ability to listen for both what is and isn't being said, noticing body language and facial expressions, changes in tone of voice, and even shifts of energy. It's also about listening for the small stuff, the big stuff, and all the stuff in between.

Empathizing. Empathy is not about feeling sorry for clients. Empathy is, in a very crude way, "sitting in the shit" with clients and acknowledging the feelings they are experiencing. Whether as the coach or client, we all recognize that life isn't always a bowl of cherries and it can sometimes feel like all you are getting is the pits. Being willing to sit with clients as they work through a tough situation (perhaps losing a contract they expected to win, the loss of a key employee, or a project taking a bad turn) and not trying to fix their mood or minimize the situation is important in supporting clients to greater resiliency and resourcefulness.

Questioning. Earlier in this book, I discussed how to use a journalistic view to ask questions to get to the core of an issue—who, what, where, when, why, and how—and that is applicable in coaching as well. In coaching, I ask powerful questions that encourage clients to go deeper, and that invite clarity, discovery, and action. For example, I might ask a client who isn't getting the most effort out of an employee questions like: "What assumptions are you making about your employee?" or "How might you be contributing to this situation?" or "What approaches have worked in the past?" As the coach, you are asking the question, not answering it or offering an opinion or solution.

Giving feedback. Feedback is often viewed through the lens of assessing performance. That feedback could be of a manager to an employee, a client to a contractor, or a prime contractor to a subcontractor. In the context of coaching, the feedback takes on a different flavor. The feedback we are talking about is reflecting the comments clients have made (think about it as a coach holding up a mirror) and acknowledging what has been shared. A typical example of this could be a coach starting a sentence with, "So what

I'm hearing is . . . Is that accurate?" or "First off, congratulations on
. . ." That lets clients know they are being heard.

Intuiting. Intuition can be a funny thing. Gavin de Becker is
widely considered the leading expert on the protection of public
figures and his work on the prediction and prevention of violence
has earned him three Presidential appointments. He is also the
best-selling author of *The Gift of Fear: Survival Signs that Protect
Us from Violence*. As a security expert, de Becker cautions that
most of us are not good about listening to our own intuition. We
assume the best and ignore the risks. From a coaching perspective,
this can take the form of listening to the various parts of the
conversation, listening for what is left unsaid, and piecing together
a bigger picture. While clients may not explicitly say, "I have a
value around hard work and a strong work ethic," coaches may
hear the description and the conversation and say, "It sounds to me
like you may not be taking time to recharge your batteries and do
something just for yourself. What do you think about that?"

Checking. The idea of checking can take a number of forms, and
in my work as a coach, I often use this concept to check in with
clients to make sure we are still on target or ensure I understand
the situation as explained. This could be asking for examples of
how the situation presents itself or for clarification (i.e., "When
you use the word 'integrity,' what does that mean to you?").

Is this the complete list? No, but by gaining a little understanding about what coaching is all about, you may be able to use some of these skills to develop a deeper relationship with your employees. You may also be thinking that starting a relationship with a coach would provide some benefits, personally and professionally. It is also important to realize that a coaching relationship is highly personal, so I would not recommend you jump right in and start working with the first person you find. Most coaches, as part of an exploratory conversation, will actually provide some coaching so you can get a sense if there is a good fit. In addition to finding a good fit from a personality perspective, it is important to have a sense of what you are struggling to overcome (i.e., leadership, performance, management, communications) and ask potential coaches about their experience dealing with those issues as well as their understanding of your industry or organizational type.

What Is Mentoring?

There are differences between mentoring and coaching, though a mentor can still employ a coaching approach in the relationship to dig deeper, elicit clarity, and actively listen to the protégé.

Mentoring is also future-focused but differs from coaching in two fundamental ways. Mentors share their own personal experience and professional path as an example of successes and failures. Mentors also open doors for their mentees, making introductions and connecting them to others within their networks who can help them along the professional journey. Many large organizations have formal mentor–protégé programs that pair older and more established staff with new or junior staff to help ease them into the organization, explain how things work (the things that don't appear in the employee handbook), or help them understand the corporate culture. Mentoring is typically semi-structured guidance where mentors share their knowledge, skills, and experience to assist protégés to progress in their own lives and careers. Mentors need to be readily accessible and prepared to offer help as the need arises—within agreed bounds. In many organizations with formal programs, there is a matching process and an expectation that the mentor and protégé will meet with some regularity.

Mentoring is really more than giving advice or passing on what your experience was in a particular area or situation. There can be a tendency for mentors to launch into old war stories about how things were done back in the day, even if the situations have radically changed. When I began my career, we had shared computers and drafting tables for project plans, and computer drafting was not yet in vogue. In fact, as I mentioned earlier, my work neighbor was an eighty-five-year-old Hungarian who likely had forgotten more about engineering than I would ever know—but he was not the mentoring type, despite the decades of experience. He was about the past and could not reconcile with the changes coming in the industry that would ultimately eliminate his job.

Mentoring is about motivating and empowering other people to identify their own issues and goals, and helping them to find ways of resolving or reaching them—not by doing it for them, or expecting them to "do it the way I did it,"—but by understanding and respecting different ways of working. As you might imagine, the coaching approach of asking powerful questions can be an integral part of the mentoring process, with a very key difference: mentors are invested in the person, their path, and a particular outcome. Coaching is a more neutral process where the coach is invested in the person, but not in a particular path, approach, or outcome. Mentors say, "here's how *I* did it," while coaches ask, "how would *you* like to do it?"

The question that often comes up is "why would someone agree to be a mentor?" The answer: because the commitment can be key to the professional development and advancement of their junior colleagues. It's the same reason I take phone calls and give advice when a contractor calls with a thorny question: generosity—of time, spirit, experience, and expertise. Some think of mentoring as paying it forward because someone in their past took the time to provide some mentoring, or they cast it in the light of giving back to their industry, alma mater, or former colleagues. For me, it comes with a sense of pride that an individual or business owner would ask for input, advice, or guidance. I was fortunate to have had both good and bad examples to draw from as a way to formulate my own approach to mentoring. After almost thirty years in the engineering and construction industry, I can still pick up the phone and call a former boss or colleague to kick around some ideas I'm struggling with. Mentorship can be a short-term arrangement, but the development of that relationship allows you to quickly pick up the conversation even though months or years have passed between calls.

There are also some people I have known professionally who considered themselves mentors, but the level of mentorship involved the here-is-what-you-should-do approach. This leads to a generally unsatisfying feeling, as opposed to asking "how can I help and what are you trying to deal with?"

In the context of mentoring and what you can expect as a protégé, or as you are thinking long term about how you might want to be a mentor, here are some things to remember:

Advice does not have to be implemented exactly as it's given. Providing advice can be a key part of a mentoring relationship as long as the advice is asked for and comes from a genuine place of wanting the best for the person you are mentoring. Even if it is genuine, the mentee may decide to go in a different direction, take bits and pieces, or implement exactly as given. As a mentor, it is important to not take it personally even though you are invested in the outcome. If the consequences of the decision are fully considered, you have to let your mentee take the reins of the decision.

No two experiences are the same. As was discussed above, try avoiding the "back in the day" comparisons to your mentee's situation, particularly with junior professionals who are trying to figure it all out and create their own personas and philosophies. The experiences you share should be relevant, useful, and timeless. I often share my experiences as to how I made decisions (e.g., *Do I go to graduate school for engineering or business? When did I know it was time to look for a new challenge? How did I assess corporate culture?*) or how I dealt with challenging work situations. Helping your protégé recognize the process elements allows that person to fill in the color based on your experience and results.

Pick up the phone on behalf of your mentee. In general, successful professionals do not get there purely on their own—there were people along the way willing to make an introduction, get their information in front of the right person, or generally advocate on their behalf. That being said, mentees shouldn't expect the mentor to do their bidding and get them into a situation they don't deserve or can't successfully handle. That reflects on the mentor and the mentee, and credibility is key for both. I get many phone calls that start with "Do you know someone who does x, y or z?" or "Can you put me in touch with someone at this company?" I am likely to agree to do so once I have a little more information about purpose. I still—using my coaching skills—get them to clarify what they want and in what form to be targeted.

Intergenerational workplaces have turned mentoring on its head. Traditionally, mentors were the more senior and mentees or protégés were more junior, but in a number of ways, that dynamic is changing. The rapidly changing nature of industry often puts the junior staff in the driver's seat when it comes to innovation and technology. In construction, contractors are no longer figuring estimates on the back of a paper bag, and the competitive nature of the industry has given rise to the use of websites, social media, and the like. In an ideal world, the junior staff would be mentoring the older staff on the use of technology, new ways of thinking, or different approaches to workplace issues. The benefit of this approach is greater engagement and investment—the junior staff will likely see themselves as being valued, respected, and integral to the future of the organization—and none of those are bad things, right?

What Is Consulting And Is It Worth The Money?

Earlier in the book, I described situations when the most appropriate answer to a question is, "It depends," and this question is really no different. Before digging deeper into the question, let's clarify the nature of consulting and when it might be the tool you are looking for to address your business needs.

As a small business owner, it is important to recognize what consultants are and are not as it relates to your overall operation. Consultants are generally your subject matter experts; they have expertise in an area currently not covered by existing staff, or in one that does not support the idea of hiring a full-time employee.

Think of a consultant as your temporary resource to help solve a specific challenge. Please note the more active nature being described, because the consultant actually completes tasks based on an agreed-upon scope of work, where a mentor may point you in a specific direction, and a coach would help you figure out which direction you want and need to go.

There are some examples of consulting that come up frequently with growing companies that have not fully matured to the point of having an expansive infrastructure to support the business's operations and goals. When you are talking about creating a business plan—not for the purpose of selling the business but to clarify the path forward and perhaps for loan applications—a consultant is an excellent choice. Similarly, the evaluation of your HR function as it relates to employee handbooks, benefits packages, job descriptions, and recruiting is an opportunity to bring in a consultant. A consultant will be able to help assess your organizational structure and highlight gaps in staffing or future needs.

The advantage of consulting is the ability to look at situations in a clinical and clean manner, since the consultant is not emotionally invested in the company or the outcome. With the wrong consultant, that can be the greatest detriment as well. In many respects, using consulting as a means to support your business growth is having the clarity to understand what you need, when you need it, and in what way you would like the support.

Remember, in this case, you are the client. As you think about the relationship you have with your clients and the manner in which they hold you to a specific scope of work, you have to now put the client hat on, which means guarding against scope creep (don't let the phrase "while you're here …" appear—that means dollar signs for a contractor or consultant), managing the deliverables, and associated costs. Many, if not all, of you who are reading this book have responded to RFPs, RFQs, or invitations to bid on projects, and a similar approach would be advised when you are considering consulting as the avenue for supporting your business.

As a small business owner, here are some concepts to keep in mind as you look to hire a consultant:

First is not best. Don't hire the first consultant who comes along. This seems like a self-defeating recommendation when I myself am a consultant, but reputable consultants will recognize there needs to be a good fit from a relationship perspective to mesh with a client. Is it the most important element? Not necessarily, but if you don't like who you are working with, how hard are you going to work for their success? Once you have a good handle on the support you need, get it down on paper so the conversations you have with potential consultants will result in consistent proposals—you are comparing apples to apples, not bananas. As a consultant, I am never offended or put off by a potential client who responds at a meeting with "we need to think about it" or "we have a few others to speak to," because it indicates seriousness and thoroughness. We talked about managing your sales funnel in the chapter on marketing; consultants do the same thing and do not expect every conversation or proposal to result in a contract. Be professional, respectful of their time, and transparent. In other words, follow the Golden Rule and treat them the way you would want to be treated.

Experience matters. Would you hire a plumber to install a fire sprinkler system who had only been working in the residential market renovating bathrooms? Probably not. As you clarify the specific needs you would like the consultant to help with, look for those with relevant experience and expertise. Honest consultants will tell you if something is outside their area of expertise, and will provide examples of their work and references you can call. I recently got into a conversation with a company about helping with a complicated certification issue. The person I was speaking with said, "well, this is something you can help us with," and was a little surprised when I declined. I knew enough to give general guidance and identify some of the pertinent issues, but what the company really needed was an attorney specializing in this area to advise them. You are the client; don't be shy about expecting a consultant to demonstrate relevant or comparable experience, expertise, and industry knowledge.

Expect privacy. The likelihood is your company is not developing a proprietary technology application you want to keep out of the public sphere. However, you also don't want your personal or company details splashed across the front of *The New York Times* or given to an existing or potential client. When you are thinking about using a consultant, you should expect privacy and confidentiality, since you will likely be sharing information about finances, employee performance, legal complications, insurance or bonding challenges, project disputes, or loan applications. When I meet with potential clients for the first time, I reassure them that everything we talk about is confidential, and if it progresses to an actual engagement, I am never opposed to signing a nondisclosure agreement (NDA). In fact, I am frequently surprised when the request does not come. Do not hesitate to ask for an NDA, and again, a reputable consultant will not balk. It protects you and your company. Your attorney should be able to draft an NDA for your purposes, or reach out to your network/trade associations to see if they have one that will serve your needs.

OK, but how much will it cost? Pricing for a consultant can be structured in a number of ways, and in certain respects, it may come down to the level of investment that fits the overall budget. Three of the most common options will be hiring a consultant on 1) an hourly rate, 2) a project basis, or 3) a monthly retainer.

For some activities that may be longer-term engagements without clean and clear delineations, you can hire a consultant at an hourly rate. You will pay more per hour for a consultant than hiring a

196 BUILD LIKE THE BIG PRIMES

full-time employee, but the ability to phase a consultant in and out without HR complications or for a very specific need works to your advantage. As you are comparing pricing for a number of consultants, remember that cheapest is not always the best. You should weigh their individual experiences in the industry, expertise for the task you need completed, their references, and perhaps most importantly, your comfort working with the person. As a business owner, and a consistent theme I hear from my clients, you do not want to be judged on the low-bid concept and I would advise against that in selecting a consultant too. What is the best value available?

Another option is to develop a neat and concise scope of work and hire the consultant on a project basis, as you would expect when hired by one of your clients. The agreed-upon scope and price allow you to get the services you need and the consultant will work as efficiently as possible to produce the results or deliverables. It will be important to build in a contingency rate for activities that may extend beyond the base agreement. A typical instance is the request to attend a meeting with a potential client or agency that had not been anticipated. The consultant may be able to accommodate it within the project budget, but if not, having a set hourly rate will facilitate the process.

A third option is to hire a consultant on a retainer basis if there is an expectation of long-term needs and the consultant has the breadth and scope of knowledge to advise and deliver in multiple areas. This can get a little tricky, but is worth considering. It does require an agreement on the limits of service (for example, x number of meetings, unlimited email access, x number of hours to draw from, etc.), but provides an alternative to a pure hourly rate. It can alleviate the fear of picking up the phone because of the cost and will likely result in a discounted hourly rate from the consultant. If you decide to go the retainer route, use the hours. Don't leave resources on the table, since most consultants will expect a use-it-or-lose-it arrangement and may want a commitment of a six-month contract.

On the page in black and white, it is all clean and sterile and neat. In reality, there can be a lot of overlap among the three concepts, and having a better understanding of each will be instructive in identifying which you actually need. As a small business consultant, I often use coaching techniques to draw clients into a deeper conversation—they may not distinguish between coaching and consulting, but I do, and it can be a seamless transition between the two. The important factor to consider, whether you are looking for a coach, mentor, or consultant, is to make sure there is a good fit (would you want to meet them for coffee?), the industry experience is relevant (you might not want to work with someone who does not understand the lingo), there is expertise in delivering similar projects, and you trust the person.

As a coach, mentor, and consultant, I have to be conscious of the conversations I am having with clients and how conversations can quickly shift, necessitating my taking off one hat and putting on another. For example, I wear my consultant hat when a client needs a business plan or strategic marketing plans, or a review of financial statements. I wear my coach hat when a client (owners, managers and staff) is looking to explore personal and professional opportunities that could include leadership and communication issues, business growth, or a career shift. And wearing my mentor hat, I help clients make a connection with a particular company or to another client that can help them become known, make a pitch for their services, or explore opportunities to partner on a particular project.

4X4 IN COACHING, MENTORING, AND CONSULTING

What does it mean to be a 4x4 performer as it pertains to coaching, mentoring, and consulting in your personal and professional life?

 Competence relates to awareness and willingness to consider performance factors and needs beyond the delivery of projects. As the owner or manager, this cuts two ways: are you aware of your needs and open to getting the proper help and the proper time and are you attentive to those who work with and for you so you can appropriately support them?

Qualified in this regard goes to your ability to find the most qualified person or company to provide the needed services. As with most industries, there are qualifications and certifications for coaches and I would encourage you to start with a coach certified through an organization like the International Coach Federation.

 Responsive contractors do not take a "hands off" or "wait and see and hope it gets better on its own" attitude. In this regard, responsiveness goes to the heart of movement and recognition of needs. It can be seen as being responsive to the needs of your employees, your network, your family, and achieving your business and personal goals.

 Responsible contractors or business owners need to understand the power of coaching and mentoring and that the relationship is only as strong as the sense of responsibility each shares in its maintenance. Recognize the sensitivity of the conversations, the discretion needed to continue those conversations, and the trust that develops in both directions. Responsible owners and managers distinguish among the needs and employ the right tool for the right job.

CORNERSTONE QUESTIONS TO SUPPORT YOUR SUCCESS:

- What could the impact be if you listened more? What might you hear from your employees that could support the growth of the company and meet their development needs?

- How have you seen these concepts throughout your career? How did it feel to be coached or mentored? What would it be like to have someone else feel that way through your actions?

- What challenges, dilemmas, and opportunities would you bring to coaching, mentoring, or consulting? What support do you need to fully realize your potential, facilitate your growth, and exceed your professional goals?

CHAPTER 11

Work-Life Balance: You're More Than Just Your Business

©Glasbergen

"I'm successful in business because I'm lucky.
But I didn't get lucky until I started working 90 hours a week!"

We casually throw around the term "work-life balance" as if it is easy to attain. In truth, it might be the most challenging aspect of being a small business owner. Throughout the previous ten chapters we have talked about all manner of situations that require choices around how to spend your time and effort, though almost exclusively as it relates to your work life. In all honesty, the to-do list never ends. If I granted you a 25th hour of the day to dedicate to work activities, you would find things to do. Invoicing, reviewing financial reports, returning phone calls or email, scheduling coffee or a client meeting, attending an industry breakfast or dinner, maybe even just cleaning up your desk. I'm right there with you—and this does not even address the pressing priorities.

If you are like me, you have other things outside of work that satisfy you, relax you, and bring you joy. I recharge my batteries by spending time with my wife and our sweet rescued pit bull, Nash, baking bread to eat and to give away to friends and family, going to the gym, talking to my kids about their days at college, or catching up on the latest episode of *The Profit*, *American Pickers*, or *Dirty Jobs* on the DVR.

But being able to do those enjoyable activities (or do nothing at all for a few hours) and still run a business takes planning, discipline, and commitment. And without that, you run the risk of burnout, which can lead to some irreparable problems for you and your business.

Recognize Burnout *Before* You Burn Out

Burnout may occur when you've been working without a break to give yourself the time *and* headspace to recharge. This is true for your employees as well. According to a Gallup study of nearly 7,500 full-time employees, about two-thirds of full-time workers experience burnout on the job. And the organizational costs are significant, with burned-out employees being 63 percent more likely to take a sick day, more than twice as likely to be looking for a new job, and are 23 percent more likely to visit the emergency room.

For the health and well-being of yourself, your family, your team, *and* your business, you need to catch the signs of burnout early. According to David Ballards, head of The American Psychological Association's Psychologically Healthy Workplace Program, here are ten signs that you're experiencing burnout:

 Exhaustion: You're tired all the time.

 Lack of Motivation: Things that used to engage, excite or drive you no longer do.

 Frustration, Cynicism and Other Negative Emotions: You've become a pessimist, and can no longer find the silver lining in difficult situations.

 Cognitive Problems: You're having trouble paying attention and concentrating.

 Slipping Job Performance: Your work just isn't of the same quality that it was a few months ago.

 Interpersonal Problems at Home and at Work: You're fighting more or you're withdrawing more.

7. **Not Taking Care of Yourself:** You're eating or drinking too much, not sleeping enough, skipping the gym, etc.

8. **Being Preoccupied With Work...When You're Not at Work:** Your mind never shuts off, even when you're not working.

9. **Generally Decreased Satisfaction:** Everything just feels...blah.

10. **Health Problems:** You're getting sick more often than you used to—and more often than you should or can afford to.

Because burnout can creep up slowly—it's all too easy to make the leap from a few bad days to complete burnout—it's important to recognize it before it becomes permanent.

Here are some of the strategies I use in my own life, and that I share with my clients:

Make Your Calendar Your Friend

Schedule spontaneity. Yes, I mean it. It sounds like a strange concept but you will be much more likely to spend time away from work doing the things you like to do if you put them in your calendar. Write it down, put it someplace where others can see it, and find an accountability partner. I'm not advocating that your calendar has to be written out to account for all 24 hours of the day—16 if you plan on getting some sleep—but if there is a movie you want to see or a concert to attend, make sure you put it down in ink and invite whoever you want to join you.

When our kids were much younger, my wife and I would schedule date nights to ensure we got an occasional break. We loved our kids (and still do) but there were times that we just needed to escape for some adult conversation. If you have ever had young kids there is always something to do—cleaning up, washing dishes, laundry, food shopping, etc. As much as you love your kids, and your business may feel like a child, you do need a break or you will not be helpful to your employees, partners, clients, or your family.

Unplug

Nearly any newspaper or magazine article or story on TV that focuses on technology eventually talks about screen addiction—not just in adolescents and teens, but also in adults. The near-constant connectedness that comes with the "hard plastic rectangle" (as Jerry Seinfeld jokes about in his stand-up routine) means that if you don't make a conscious choice to unplug there will come a time where you feel like you can't.

I recently delivered a Time Management workshop, and one of the participants talked about how early in his career he left the office at 5:00 p.m. and there were no expectations of calls or emails until the following work day. We seem to have lost that luxury of time to recover from the busyness of the day but it is important to watch for the warning signs. My daughter will grab an empty bread basket when the extended family comes for dinner and insists on everyone dropping in their cell phones. It is met with resistance, reluctance, and some dirty looks—and yet, everyone complies. For at least an hour, we all re-engage, have conversation, share funny (and sad) memories, and participate in some good-natured teasing. The other bit of advice that I wish I were more consistent at doing is to not have my cell phone charging on my nightstand. When I do, it means that the last thing I see at night and the first thing I see in the morning is my cell phone. The ding or buzz of an email, text message, or social media alert has turned us all into one of Pavlov's dogs—we can't help but reach for the "hard plastic rectangle."

Get More And Better Sleep

I recall (or at least I wish I could recall) the semester in business school when I was going to school full time, working full time, and my twins were newly born and had to be fed every three hours around the clock. There was not enough caffeine in the entire Starbucks empire that could have made me awake enough to competently attend to all those needs. I recently had lunch with my classmates and I once again thanked them for carrying me through a semester (and to be honest, I don't even know what classes I took).

Lack of sleep over a protracted period has some unbelievably negative impacts on a person physically and mentally. At a certain point, lack of sleep will indeed mimic the symptoms of drinking alcohol. When I worked for the utility company and dealt with construction crews arriving by 7:00 a.m., I was routinely at my desk by 6:00 a.m. to prepare for the day which meant I was getting out of bed at 4:30 a.m. or, as my wife called it, "dark o'clock."

The best advice we got as new parents was "sleep when the babies sleep" and for you as a business owner that can be interpreted as "take advantage of the lulls in the business" to get the sleep you need. Most doctors recommend getting eight hours of sleep every night. You may be the kind of person who seems to get by on five hours sleep, but is drinking too many cups of coffee. Most importantly, be aware of the warning signs like the general lack of energy, the dark rings under the eyes, the 3:00 p.m. coffee run, a certain irritability with employees, friends or family, or perhaps an inattention to detail that is not customary, but is becoming costly.

Delegate What You Can To Take Back Your Time

One of the hardest things to do for a business owner or manager is to let go of certain activities and delegate. This happens in our personal lives as much as it happens in our professional lives. On the personal side, there are opportunities to find the help you need to get a little time back for yourself and to foster the important relationships. This might include hiring a babysitter once or twice a month so you can go out for dinner and a movie (and I'm sure there are some high school or college kids in your neighborhood who would love to get paid to watch tv and eat your snacks). Perhaps bringing in a cleaning service would take some responsibilities off your plate and provide a little breathing room. In your business, it may involve an intern who can do research for you or a part-time employee to do your filing or bookkeeping. In the spirit of working *on* your business more and *in* your business less, identify those tasks that someone else can do…and block off the time for yourself.

Remember Who's In Charge Of Your Work And Life: You!

Being a small business owner means that you have the ability and authority to make many decisions about how you spend your time. The thing that drove you to become an entrepreneur can easily take you so far down the rabbit hole of work that you begin neglecting relationships and self-care. In the rough and tumble world of construction, self-care is not a regularly talked about concept (and I am not talking about getting a new pair of work boots as an act of self-care). Self-care is managing your "neck up" conditions and ensuring you can continue to be helpful and supportive to those in your personal and professional lives. Consider your mental health in the same context as you would job site safety. If you walk the job site looking for potential OSHA violations or trip hazards, also be mindful of the warning signs of burnout, depression, or anxiety in yourself and others. Don't let anyone try and convince you that mental health is not important. Your mood and frame of mind are every bit as important to your performance and productivity as your physical health. And that's not just for you—that's for your entire team.

If Work Were Always Fun It Would Be Called Play

It is important to acknowledge that, while you may love being a business owner and spending time with the crews, sometimes it just sucks. The work is piling up, the phone keeps ringing, the inbox has way too many unanswered emails, and you find yourself snapping at whoever crosses your path regardless of the situation. It has happened to us all (my kids would testify that they can recognize the look in my eyes and have been on the receiving end of a few loud responses, grunts, or glares). While it's not something to be ashamed of, it is something that requires your attention sooner rather than later.

Don't get me wrong: I love being my own boss (well, aside from my wife and dog who *really* run the show) and there is nothing better than a great compliment from a client, an excited email from a colleague, or getting the call that you've won a project you pursued. The rest of the time, you have to figure out how to remember the joy that you find in your work and the reason you are working long hours day in and day out. If you are feeling this way then there is almost a guarantee that your employees sometimes feel similarly.

When December rolls around there are often too many invitations to holiday parties than any one person could possibly attend. Take the opportunity to do something with your team throughout the year that lets them blow off the steam. A happy hour in March before the days get longer might help you and your staff through the winter doldrums and remind everyone that you all generally like each other.

Will there ever really be balance? Not unless you are conscious of what is happening around you, to you, and within you. I suspect you may continue to display all the characteristics of a workaholic as you are building for the future and potentially a legacy. That's OK, as long as you carve out the time to do the things that make you feel a little more relaxed, a little more human, a little more balanced.

4X4 IN WORK-LIFE BALANCE

What does it mean to be a 4x4 performer when you consider your overall work-life balance?

 Competent business owners keep their eyes open to the impact on the work-life balance of their employees and themselves. Developing the ability to even recognize those impacts is necessary and important because you have to identify the problem before you can begin to solve it. Competence also considers the proactive attitude that a business owner needs to think prospectively about what impacts to work-life balance are possible and probable.

 Qualified contractors and business owners use the tools at their disposal to address impacts to work-life balance and support others in maintaining that balance. They also have developed a system for themselves where they can be alert, aware, rested, and approachable.

 Responsiveness may seem like the opposite of being proactive but the true sense is that of addressing the needs of employees and oneself. In this regard, the business owner has to be aware of the *what* (that things are getting unbalanced) but also the *how* (the means and methods to tip the scales back).

 Responsible business owners understand the concept of not asking others to do what they would not be willing to do *and* demonstrate that they take that idea seriously in their own lives. If you are responsible in promoting work-life balance, consider refraining from emailing employees on nights and weekends. If you do, all of the talk will be for naught once you demonstrate your own true attitudes.

CORNERSTONE QUESTIONS TO SUPPORT YOUR SUCCESS:

- How would you describe your current risk of burnout? How would you describe the current risk of burnout for your employees? What would the impact be of ignoring the risks? What would the impact be of getting ahead of it?

- What are the triggers that can instantly put you in a bad mood? How can you begin to recognize them before they take over?

- What are the activities that you can incorporate to relieve the tension, lower the pressure, and breathe a little bit easier? Who would you like to spend more time with outside of work (no shop talk!) who you have not spent time with lately?

- What do you need to start doing differently to become the kind of boss who is aware of and actively asks employees how they feel, how they're doing, and what kind of support they need? Who does that for you?

AFTERWORD

When I teach workshops on Decision Making, I remind the participants that there is no one solution, but that a system, *any* system, applied consistently, will yield benefits. This book isn't the only system, but it highlights one system that I have found helpful to my clients—and that I use myself as a small business owner.

One final pop-culture reference: A favorite movie of mine is *City Slickers*, starring Billy Crystal as Mitch Robbins, a wise-cracking urbanite, and Jack Palance as Curly, a weathered cowboy driving cattle across the southwest. In a teaching moment, Curly holds up his index finger and asks Mitch, "What's this?" Confused,

Mitch can't answer the question, and Curly explains that his finger represents the *one thing* that is important to him—and that Mitch will have to figure out for himself what that one thing would be for his life.

For me, my *one thing* was realizing that not only could I help others but that I felt compelled to follow through on that confluence of skills, understanding, compassion, and calling.

How would you respond to Curly if he held up one finger and put the question to you? What's your one thing?

And now for some final thoughts on the *Build Like The Big Primes* system:

Finance

You are in business to make money, but that is not the only measure of success. Know your audience, refine your story, know your numbers and get comfortable having those conversations.

Operations

There will always be a lot of moving parts and a pull to get involved in every project. As the business owner you have to strike the right balance of working *in* the business and working *on* the business.

Communications

Say what you mean and mean what you say. Be truthful, open, and forthright in your communications with clients, employees, vendors, and service providers. Communicate early and often.

Branding

As the business owner you are the face of the company and in many cases the reason you have been awarded a contract. Remember *The New York Times* rule: don't damage your reputation by doing something you'd be ashamed to have printed in big, bold letters.

Marketing

Shakespeare wrote, "To thine own self be true," and this is a perfect quote for your marketing efforts. Know what you can and can't do and be willing to say "no" if the opportunity is outside your lane.

Human Resources

People are the linchpin to your success or failure. Without labor you will not be able to perform and treating your staff fairly and respectfully will likely turn you from a small contractor to a preferred employer for high quality employees.

Coaching, Mentoring, And Consulting

Listen more and talk less and be generous with your time. Someone likely took the time to do both when you were starting out and, even if not, set yourself apart from others by supporting others and being willing to ask for the right kind of help and the time that you need it.

Work-Life Balance

Unfortunately, there is no silver bullet to solve the challenge of getting overwhelmed by the demands of the business. Keep a reminder around about why you became a business owner and find a relief valve that will allow you to remain productive, effective, and smiling. You are not only entitled to take care of your physical and mental health—you are obligated to. You have people depending on you.

4x4 Performance

It will be important in business to remember that you have to be competent, qualified, responsive, and responsible. Regardless of the tool you are considering or a situation outside of work, this 4x4 concept can be applied.

Competent

You need to have the basic abilities to actually perform the work you've been contracted to do. Developing a basic level of competence will be critical before moving onto more advanced concepts. Put yourself in a growth mindset where you are open to learning and incorporating new skills.

Qualified

Do you have the credentials to deliver on what you are pursuing or promising? It will always be better to underpromise and overperform than overpromise and underperform. And if you are not yet qualified, figure out what it will take to become qualified, and work with others who are qualified until you get there.

Responsive

Responsiveness has to do with timeliness, managing expectations, and completeness. It is important to reply to calls and emails in a reasonable period and empty your voicemail box in case a client calls and wants to leave a message.

Responsible

Overcommitment can make you seem like you lack the level of responsibility to deliver as promised. Honesty will go a long way to developing the reputation of being responsible—responsible with a client's trust, an agency's money, or your employees' safety.

Looking back over a career now spanning more than thirty years, I marvel at the good fortune I have had to work with amazing people who have influenced my career, taken me under their wing, guided me, and worked beside me to allow me to be the coach, mentor, and consultant I have become. And looking to the future allows me to imagine what can be, who I will have the opportunity to help and influence, the positive impact I can have, and the chance to further hone my craft in the service of my clients. My wish for you is my take on the lyrics of the 1986 hit song by Timbuk 3, that "your future's so bright, you gotta wear shades!"

(OK, I guess I had one last pop-culture reference in me!)

I hope this book is just the start of our relationship. I look forward to your thoughts, comments, challenges, and arguments, but most of all, I hope you will let me know how you are progressing toward your goals. And if I can be of help as a coach, consultant, or mentor (or all three) don't hesitate to email, call, or visit my website at www.AECBusinessStrategies.com.

My phone number can be found on my website, and my email address is MRiegel@AECBusinessStrategies.com.

Michael Riegel

APPENDIX

Acknowledgments

When I started this process, I had no idea what I was doing except for the fact that I had this idea. My wife, Deborah, has been along for the entire journey, all the way back to the early days of my career, and has always been my biggest cheerleader. She understood what I was trying to say, and I used her as my model (although she is a far superior writer), but she will admit she leans on me to help keep her organized. I could not have even considered the idea of writing a book, becoming a consultant, or going back to school without her unwavering support.

My parents have been unbelievable role models and without their love, guidance, and support I would not be who I am nor would I have been able to accomplish much of what I have. To my dad who stressed the importance of math, "second acts," and being your own boss—thank you, thank you, thank you. It might not have been dental school, but I could not have imagined it turning out better. And to my mom who never let me get away with lax writing, poor grammar, and gave me the detail-focus that has served me well— your contributions to my success can never be repaid. The lessons of integrity, responsibility, and commitment to one's word are life lessons I carry with me always and have done my best to pay it forward to the next generation.

This book would also not have been possible without some excellent role models, bosses, and colleagues throughout the past quarter century. Martin Taub and Paul Eng-Wong provided the example I needed to learn about stretching beyond my limits, thinking bigger, and the idea of true mentorship and integrity. I credit them both with instilling in me *The New York Times* rule and will forever fear Marty's felt tip pen edits. Mike Ruiz has been a friend, colleague, and confidant for nearly fifteen years, and I remain grateful to him for giving me the space to explore professionally, partnering with me on some odd projects, and allowing me to acquire some valuable tools. In retrospect, my time working for and with Mike were some of the most productive, influential, and informative years in my career. Ann Farrell has been my personal and professional coach and supported my efforts to become a certified coach. She has been masterful at helping me "figure it out" and often reminded me to trust my instincts, even when I wanted to give advice.

Jacob and Sophie, our Wonder Twins, have often been the driving force for me to do better as a father and as a consultant. Invariably, I have been the one working from home who gets wrangled into helping manage and build school projects. What this affords me (in addition to getting to work in my gym clothes many days) is the opportunity to impart a little wisdom to the kids along the way—some through bad jokes, some conversations about baseball with Jacob, and some deep discussions about statistics—until Sophie left me in the dust. I am pretty sure I learned as much from them as they learned from me, and after all, isn't that the way it's supposed to be?

Finally, to all the clients, contractors, colleagues, and friends throughout the years who I have been talking to about my work, their work, and the nature of construction, thank you for your patience, attention, and support. When they have asked, "How do you know that?" the answer often comes with a shrug of experience and the response, "It's not a magic trick." Were it not for you, the readers, I would not have pushed myself through the years to learn more, think harder, and get it all down on paper. I hope this book inspires you to do the same in life and in business.

About The Author

Michael Riegel is the managing director for A/E/C Business Strategies, a consulting firm that helps organizations clarify their goals, identify their challenges, and plan for their increased success. He is a coach, consultant, and project management expert with thirty years of experience working across industries delivering projects and programs for internal and external clients. Michael has developed an expertise in managing technical professionals and creating teams to deliver projects and meet organizational goals. He also enjoys leading teams through the planning, design, and execution phases of small- to large-scale projects and organization initiatives.

Michael earned his MBA at the Zicklin School of Business at Baruch College and graduated from Wentworth Institute of Technology with a bachelor's degree in construction management. He is a certified coach through the International Coach Federation, a Project Management Professional (PMP), and completed the Master Trainer program through the Association of Talent Development. He regularly consults with and advises public agencies, technical organizations, and construction firms on a variety of topics, including the development and implementation of training programs, mentor programs, business planning, and employee engagement.

Michael began and built his career on the ability to develop practical solutions to complex projects, and his clients ranged from the Metropolitan Transportation Authority's Small Business Development Program and Columbia University to New York City Small Business Services and Fox Home Team Sports. His approach to coaching, consulting, and mentoring combines his natural intellectual curiosity (to fully understand the *what* and the *why*), analytical skills (to accelerate development of options and develop a framework for goal attainment), and ability to personally connect with his clients. Michael tailors his approach to each client's individual needs and set of circumstances and lives by the motto, "What got you here won't get you there," personally and professionally.

Michael and his wife, Deborah, arc the proud parents of twins, Jacob and Sophie, who have helped hone his project management skills. If he were not a coach, Michael would be chasing natural disasters and helping communities recover from storm damage— essentially creating order out of chaos—similar to helping his clients create order in their personal and professional lives.

Michael can be contacted for coaching, consulting, workshops, speaking invitations and quantity orders of this book at: MRiegel@AECBusinessStrategies.com.